KYLIE KWONG'S SIMPLE CHINESE COOKING CLASS

Photography by

EARL CARTER

LANTERN
an imprint of
PENGUIN BOOKS

CONTENTS

INTRODUCTION

When I wrote *Simple Chinese Cooking* my aim was to demystify Chinese cooking and to make it accessible. I had come to realise that many otherwise enthusiastic cooks were reluctant to try cooking Chinese food, because they thought the ingredients were too exotic or the techniques too difficult. I decided it was high time someone wrote an easy-to-follow Chinese cookbook that would dispel the myth that Chinese cooking was not for the home cook by presenting simple recipes using everyday ingredients. I could not have been more thrilled with the response – *Simple Chinese Cooking* seems to have really struck a chord, and many people have contacted me to share their delight at being able to produce fresh and delicious Chinese meals for their family and friends so easily.

With my *Simple Chinese Cooking Class* I want to offer you more of the same – simple, authentic Chinese recipes using the best-quality fresh produce. However, I also aim to take your Chinese cooking to the next level by introducing you to some exciting new ingredients and techniques.

Most of these recipes use ingredients that are readily available at any supermarket. One of the things I love most about Chinese cooking is that you can achieve the most stunning results using the simplest of ingredients – among my favourites in this book are the deep-fried soft-boiled eggs with iceberg lettuce and chilli salt. But I also want to tempt you to venture further afield and explore the shelves of your local Chinese supermarket or grocer, where you will discover a whole new world of flavours to inspire you. Don't worry – I'm not going to fill your cupboard with endless bottles of half-used sauces and condiments, but the addition of, say, lup cheong sausage to a stir-fry or some Asian mushrooms to a soup will add a new dimension of flavour and texture that will lift your cooking from the simple to the sublime.

Of course, besides ingredients, the other vital element of good cooking is technique. So, in this book, I've included step-by-step instructions, with photographs, to help you master some of the classic Chinese cooking techniques. Before long you'll be tea-smoking oysters to toss into a stir-fry, making your own spring rolls and dumplings and confidently poaching or steaming a lobster – trust me, it's not as tricky as you think! You can also see how to season a wok properly, and how to make those delicious sticky rice parcels wrapped in bamboo leaves.

I would also like to introduce you to what I call 'investment cooking'. By this I mean those little extras that expand your repertoire and can be made in advance and then stashed away in the refrigerator for later use. Having a few homemade sauces and pickles in your fridge is like having money in the bank!

That's why I have included a whole chapter on sauces and salts. Here you will find some of the staples of the Chinese kitchen, such as spring onion–ginger sauce, sweet chilli sauce and the famous XO sauce, an intensely flavoured garlic and chilli paste that can transform anything from scallops to fried rice with its layers of flavour and complexity. In the chapter on salads and pickles, you'll learn how to pickle everything from cauliflower and zucchini through to beetroot and radishes, then how to serve the pickles and use them in other recipes. So, for example, a few slivers of pickled ginger will enhance any number of salads and stir-fries.

Another indispensable staple in the Chinese kitchen is a red braise master stock, a simple aromatic stock that forms the basis for numerous other recipes. Once you've made it, you'll wonder how you managed without it. Red braising is such a beautiful way to gently cook meat and poultry, infusing them with flavour. And the really great thing is that you only need to make red braise master stock once, as you can freeze it and re-use it indefinitely (like sourdough cultures, some master stocks have been in use for many years, with their flavour becoming deeper and more complex over time). Another classic is braised Chinese mushrooms. With a batch of these on hand, you have the makings of at least another eight simple Chinese recipes in this book, from stir-fried vegetables or lamb to steamed fish fillets. See what I mean about 'investment cooking'? A little time spent in the kitchen at the weekend or when you have a quiet evening can make supper on busy weeknights or an impromptu dinner for friends so much easier – and tastier.

I hope that you enjoy this book, and that it provides you with inspiration for many years to come. I also hope it demonstrates, once and for all, that there is nothing to be afraid of when it comes to Chinese cooking – all it takes is a passion for good food and a willingness to have a go!

EQUIPMENT

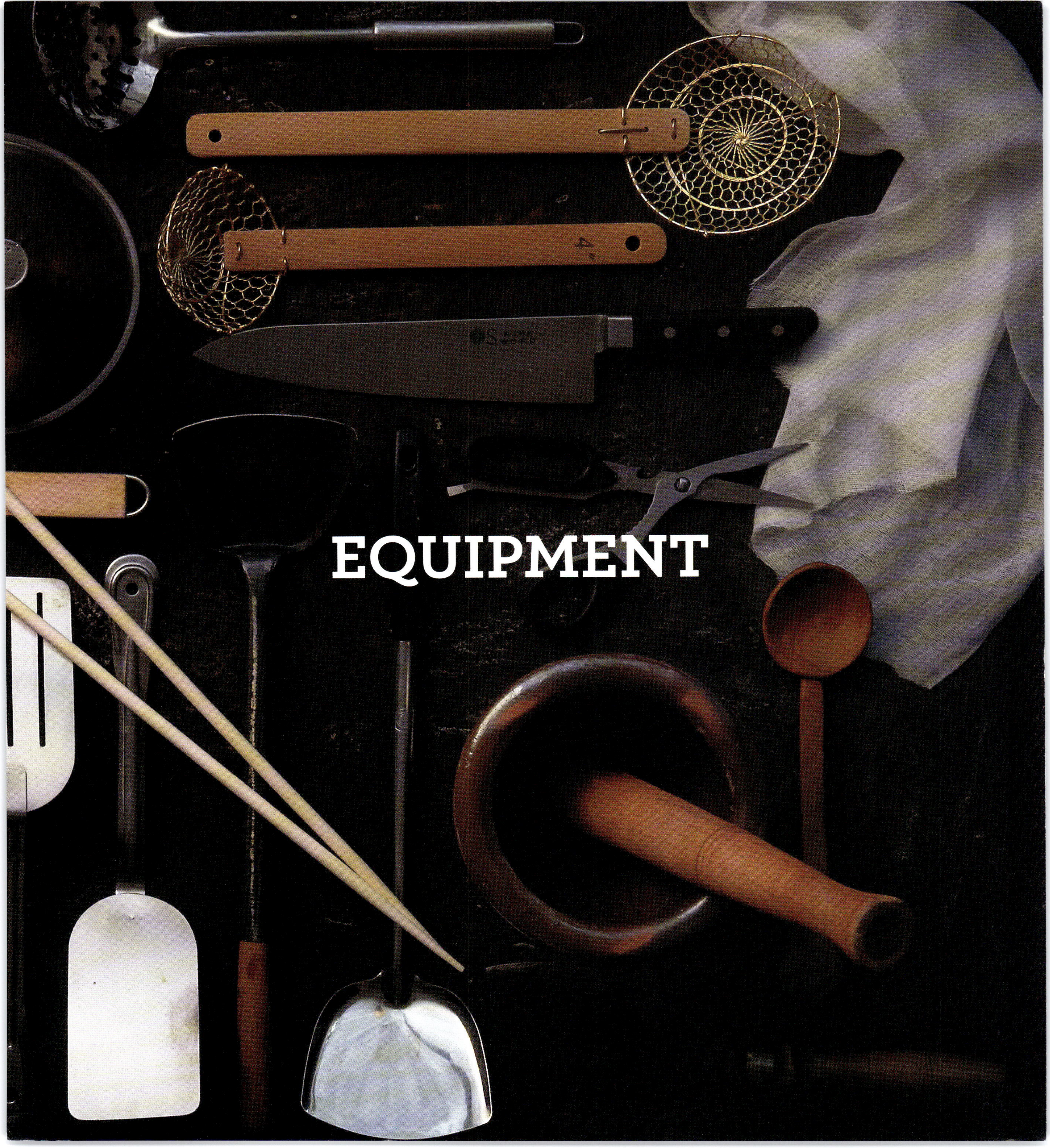

LE CREUSET

Woks

'Wok' is the Cantonese word for pot – which should give you an idea of the central place this simple utensil occupies in the Chinese kitchen.

There are various-shaped woks available, made from different materials and designed for different heat sources. The traditional round-bottomed wok is for cooking over an open flame, such as a gas stove – the round wok sides hugged by the flames act as the perfect heat conductor. Flat-bottomed woks are specifically designed for electric stoves – and are more stable, making them good for novices.

You can buy steel woks in all Chinese supermarkets. They are incredibly inexpensive and durable – just make sure you get the right size for your stove. If treated with care, it should last for years (see below for details of how to season your new wok).

Wok lids are bought separately, or you can use an ordinary saucepan lid, as long as it fits snugly within the top half of the wok.

Wok utensils

Cooking utensils to use when stir-frying in your wok include the classic shovel-shaped wok spoon, other wooden or metal spoons and spatulas, chopsticks or tongs – whatever you feel comfy with, and is appropriate to the surface of the wok.

Steamers

I think the Chinese way of steaming is brilliantly simple – a lidded basket set over a pan of boiling water. There are two types of steaming vessels, bamboo and metal. Both are inexpensive and work well, so it really comes down to personal preference.

Most of us are familiar with the traditional bamboo steamers hand-fashioned from woven bamboo. The slightly dome-shaped lid absorbs any condensation, so that no liquid drips down to waterlog the food. Bamboo steamers are sold with one lid and as many tiers of baskets as you like – or as will fit in your kitchen . . . Look out for steamers with woven lacings or ties along the side, as these indicate a strong, firm basket. With repeated use, the bamboo inevitably wears and weakens, so it helps to buy a well-made one initially – mind you, bamboo steamers are so cheap, it's not really worth losing sleep over!

In my restaurant I use metal steamers for their sheer robustness. Their other advantage is that they come with a perfect-fitting pan to hold the boiling water, whereas the bamboo steamer relies on the cook to choose a pan that suits its dimensions.

On the other hand, I use bamboo steamers at home purely for aesthetic reasons – I just love their traditional, rustic look. I could not live without my bamboo steamers – and not just for cooking Chinese food. As well as steaming any vegetables and fish to perfection, they are also excellent for reheating food, keeping rice hot, and for warming bowls and plates prior to serving a meal. They are so easy to clean: I like to wash my bamboo steamers in hot soapy water to get rid of any fishy smells and greasy, oily residues. Rinse well with boiling water, then leave to dry thoroughly, to prevent mould forming.

❶ To season a new carbon steel wok so it's ready for use, first wash it with warm soapy water and a non-metallic scourer to scrub off the greasy film that coats the wok to protect it in transit. Dry thoroughly with paper towel.

❷ Pour a little oil into the wok and use a paper towel to give the wok a good once-over, making sure all the inside surface of the wok is covered. Each time you use your wok, lightly oil it before you put it away to stop it from rusting.

❸ Over time, as you use the wok, it will turn black, and eventually will take on the distinctive patina of a well-seasoned wok.

They're also simple to store – hang them on a nail or hook in your kitchen, or neatly stack the baskets and lids. Because they're light in weight and low in price, you can afford to buy a range of sizes suitable for cooking anything from a small fish fillet or a handful of dumplings to a plate-size snapper or a whole chicken or duck.

Both types of steamer are readily available at most Chinese supermarkets and some regular supermarkets, as well as at kitchenware shops.

Chargrill pan

I like the wonderful smoky aroma and flavour chargrilling imparts. When food has been marinated in a salty-sweet marinade, the sugar or honey melts instantly in the heat, infusing it with woody, smoky notes.

If you don't have access to a barbecue, just use a chargrill pan placed on top of the stove. Buy the best you can afford – a heavy cast-iron one should last a lifetime.

Other equipment

Alongside the usual array of tongs, spatulas, metal spoons, wooden spoons, ladles, measuring cups and jugs, scales, paring knives, vegetable peelers, preparation bowls, a range of small to large saucepans and one or two 10-litre stockpots with lids, I would advise you to consider the following tools to complete your Chinese kitchen:

a **mortar and pestle**, preferably granite; I find the porcelain or clay versions a little too fragile for regular use. The granite ones are brilliant because of their density and weight, which means they can take years of intense grinding and pounding. They come in several sizes, but I suggest you buy one at least 16 centimetres diameter.

a **Chinese cleaver** is great for chopping through chicken and duck bones! Buy a cleaver as you would a regular chef's knife: ensure that the grip feels comfortable and is the right size for your hand; and that the 'weight' of the knife is appropriate to you. These two factors will directly affect the deftness with which you use the cleaver. I prefer the wooden-handled cleavers as the metal-handled ones become slippery all too easily if your hands are wet or have food on them.

a small, sharp **paring knife** for more fiddly cutting, slicing and trimming.

a swivel **vegetable peeler**, for shaving off ribbons of vegetables such as cucumber.

a large **chef's** pair of **wooden chopsticks** – these are very practical, especially when retrieving an ingredient from a wok filled with deep-frying oil – their length makes them safer, as long as you are a reasonably confident chopstick-er!

a shallow brass medium-sized **basket** or a stainless-steel '**spider**' – about 12 centimetres diameter – for scooping and draining.

a large **conical sieve** for straining stocks.

a smaller **sieve** – about 10 centimetres diameter – for finer work, such as straining chilli flakes from oil.

a **fish slice** for lifting fish, eggs and other delicate foods out of the pan without breaking them.

cartouche is a French term for a piece of paper used to cover the surface of poaching or braising food. The paper reduces evaporation and skinning of the liquid, as well as helping to keep the food submerged so that it cooks evenly. The French have a very sophisticated and precise way of creating a cartouche, which looks a little like origami! For the purposes of the recipes in this book, just tear a piece of baking paper or greaseproof paper roughly the size and shape of your pan and ensure that it covers the ingredients in the liquid.

muslin – a fine cotton cloth used by chefs to finely strain stocks and sauces. It is available at speciality kitchenware outlets and some fabric shops, but I find that a clean Chux or J-Cloth works just as well.

DICK AH PTY. LTD.
Chinese Noodle Manufacturers
新鮮沙河粉
Rice Noodles 1 kg(NET)
SOYA KING
日本豆腐
SILKEN Tofu
PASTEURISED
EGG WONTON PASTRY
GREEN FOOD PTY. LTD.
五香豆乾
FIVE SPICEBEAN CAKE
220g NET
公公麵
375g NET

INGREDIENTS

WHITE WHOLE PEPPER
Make This Your Choice
Hoyt's
NUTMEG
WHOLE
30g NET
URMERIC
POWDER
25g NET
DRIED CHILLI
CHILLIES
CRUSHED
DRIED HOT
25g NET
CORIANDER SEED
Nt 75G
SESAME
SEED
100g NET
9 320479 002239
中國特產
Chinese Specialty
SPICE POWDER
75g
CINNAMON
STICKS
15g NET
STAR
ANISE
12g NET
SICHUAN PEPPER
Nt 40g
CORIANDER
GROUND
25g NET
CUMMIN
SEED
WHOLE
25g NET

Every recipe in this book celebrates freshness and, of course, encourages buying food that is in season and therefore at its best and most plentiful. The range of fresh ingredients and Asian sauces and spices available today is astounding. Better still, more and more supermarkets are stocking organic produce, free-range eggs and poultry, and GM-free food. I urge you to be mindful of the origins of the food you purchase. Not only will this benefit our planet, but your efforts will also be repaid in terms of quality and flavour – and ultimately, your health and wellbeing.

Apple cider vinegar
This mild vinegar is made from the juice of ripe apples and matured in wooden vats. I like Melrose brand, which is available from health-food shops; because it is not filtered or pasteurised, it retains the fermentation residues and 'mother' (the culture that forms in living vinegar).

Bamboo shoots
Used extensively in Chinese, Japanese, Korean and South-East Asian food, bamboo shoots are available as spring shoots; and the smaller, yellow-coloured winter shoots, which I prefer as they are sweeter and more tender. Fresh bamboo is far superior to tinned – the crunchy shoots have a refreshing, earthy, straw-like taste and a crunchy texture. The shoots must be husked and, once cut, should be cooked straightaway, as they rapidly develop an acrid and bitter flavour. They must be blanched at least three times in boiling salted water before use (page 223).

Black cloud ear fungus
Fresh black cloud ear fungus has a beautiful velvety-smooth texture and a deep brownish-black colour. It is crunchy and refreshing when served raw in salads, and silky and slippery when cooked. Black cloud ear fungus is also available dried, but I much prefer the fresh, which is now grown in Australia and is increasingly available in supermarkets.

Bok choy
One of the most popular, versatile and well-known Chinese leafy vegetables, bok choy is available year round. It has snow-white or light-green stalks, a slightly bulbous base and green leaves with a mild, refreshing, tangy flavour.

Brown rice vinegar
Chinese cuisine uses a variety of rice vinegars, some of which can be quite harsh. I like to use naturally fermented brown rice vinegar for its depth of flavour and subtle astringency. My favourite brand is Spiral, which is made from organic brown rice and starter cultures, and contains enzymes that are beneficial for digestion.

Brown sugar
Although this is just white sugar that has had clarified molasses added to it, I like its caramelly flavour. And when I want extra depth of flavour, such as in a stock for red braising or a sauce to accompany red meat, I often use dark brown sugar.

Chillies
Chillies in Chinese cuisine are strongly associated with the fiery, spicy fare of Sichuan province, in south-western China. Interestingly enough, my Cantonese mother rarely cooked with chillies, but I have since become addicted to them! I use large red and green chillies a lot in my cooking: they are sweet and have a medium heat. In general, the smaller a chilli the hotter it is, and the seeds are often the hottest part – so if you want less heat, deseed chillies before using them. For my recipes, it's really up to you and your taste buds how many chillies you wish to add.
see also Dried chilli flakes

Chilli oil
Also called hot oil or red pepper oil, these bottles of ready-made chilli oil pack a punch. I like using it in dressings and stir-fries to give the dish a bit of a kick!

Chinese cabbage
With an oblong head 15–25 centimetres long, this cabbage has a light, sweet, delicate flavour and a crunchy texture. It can be served raw, shredded and tossed in salads, or steamed, stir-fried or braised. It is also often called Shanghai cabbage or wombok.

Choy sum
This green leafy vegetable has narrow stems and oval leaves, and is full of yellow flowers. It is bitter, with a mustard-like tang, and is delicious stir-fried, blanched or steamed.

Cinnamon quills
Cinnamon quills or sticks add a robust taste to dishes, and are an essential component of five-spice powder and of the master stock used in red braising.

Coriander
Also known as cilantro or Chinese parsley, coriander looks like a flat-leaf parsley but its flavour is unmistakably musky and citrussy. It heightens other flavours in a dish, while cutting through richness. All parts of the plant are used in Chinese cooking – if using the roots, wash them well as mud tends to stick to them.

Coriander seeds
Widely available, these round, ribbed, pale brown seeds are fragrant, with warm citrus notes. In Chinese cooking, they are used in meat-based stocks and in spiced salts to offset the richness of meat. If ground coriander is called for, either grind the seeds yourself using a spice grinder or mortar and pestle, or buy small amounts ready-ground and store in an airtight container away from light, heat and moisture.

Cornflour
Cornflour is used to create a crunchy coating on food that is to be deep-fried. In traditional Chinese cuisine, it is also often used to thicken sauces because it thickens with a clear sheen, as opposed to flour, which produces a more cloudy sauce. However, I rarely use cornflour for this purpose, preferring to allow the natural juices and sauces of a dish to speak for themselves.

Cumin seeds
Warm, earthy, pungent and sweet, cumin is commonly used in the Chinese north-western region of Xinjiang, where the cuisine is characterised by spice-infused roasted meats and kebabs. Whole or ground cumin seeds are also sometimes used in meat-based Chinese stocks to help balance the flavours.

Dried bamboo leaves
The dried leaves of the bamboo plant are used for wrapping dumplings and sticky rice parcels. Available from Asian supermarkets, they should be soaked in water before use to make them pliable.

Dried bean curd skins
These are made by heating soybean milk over hot water until it forms a skin, which is then removed and dried on a bamboo mat. Used as wrappers, the skins come packaged in large square sheets that are trimmed as required, and sometimes moistened before use. Available from Chinese supermarkets.

Dried chilli flakes
These are simply fresh chillies that have been left in the sun to dry and then pounded into flakes. The drying process intensifies the flavour, making dried chilli flakes sweet as well as fiery.

Dried Chinese mushrooms
Available in most Asian supermarkets, these dried black mushrooms need reconstituting in hot water. After soaking, trim off the woody stems, then braise the mushrooms (page 220) before adding them to stir-fries and soups for an intensely savoury flavour.

Dried scallops
Also called conpoy, these dried golden scallops are an expensive, highly prized ingredient, with specialist Chinese shops dedicated entirely to selling various grades. Used in soups, sauces and braises, their pungency and depth of flavour and aroma means that a little goes a long way, so it's worth buying the best quality available: Chinese herbal stores are a good place to look. Before use, dried scallops need to be reconstituted, either by soaking in shao hsing wine or steaming until tender.

Dried shrimp
These tiny dried shrimp have a salty, concentrated taste and a potent odour. They are usually used in soups, pastes, sauces and stir-fried dishes, where their flavour mellows on cooking and they provide a wonderful, chewy texture. They need to be soaked before using; I generally soak them in warm water for 15–20 minutes, which softens them to a chewy consistency and gets rid of any excess saltiness. However, for XO Sauce (page 298), I like to soak the dried shrimp overnight in shao hsing wine, so that the flavour of the wine penetrates the shrimps as well as softening them; I then add the shrimp-infused soaking wine to the sauce for maximum flavour.

Dried wakame seaweed
Available in health-food shops and Asian supermarkets, this seaweed is exceptionally rich in fibre and minerals, including iodine; it also acts as a natural flavour enhancer, bringing out the sweetness of foods it is cooked with. I use Spiral brand dried wakame, which I soak in cold water for 10 minutes and then drain thoroughly (the nutrient-rich soaking water is great for watering your plants). The rehydrated wakame is deliciously smooth and silky – perfect for adding to salads or stir-fries.

Eggs
Always buy free-range organic eggs if at all possible – the difference in flavour between a naturally farmed egg and a commercially farmed egg is incomparable, not to mention a healthier option. Check the use-by dates on egg cartons in the supermarkets; a quick way to gauge freshness is to pick one up: a fresh egg should feel heavy in your hand and have a clean smell. Store eggs in the fridge, still inside their carton.

Enoki mushrooms
Called 'golden needle mushroom' in China, the enoki is a mild-tasting, delicate, thin-stemmed mushroom with a tiny cap. Increasingly available in greengrocers and supermarkets, these mushrooms are used in Asian soups and stir-fries – just trim off the spongy bases first.

Fennel seeds
Widely available, these small, pale green or brown seeds have an aniseed flavour that adds an earthy note to stocks and spiced salts.

Firm tofu *see* Tofu

Fish and seafood
The one thing I will say about seafood is 'It must be eaten fresh!' With this mantra in mind, always try to purchase seafood on the day you will eat it or, at a stretch, the day before. It must be refrigerated as soon after purchase as possible – if practical, keep a small esky in the car for this purpose.

When buying whole fish, always look for clear, protruding eyes, fish that does not smell 'fishy', is light pink inside the gills and gut with no yellowy-brown tinges, has firm-textured flesh as opposed to mushy flesh, and a natural kind of 'glow' and sheen to the body.

Never buy fish fillets that have a fishy smell (fresh fish does not smell!) or are grey, yellowy or brownish in colour; fresh fish fillets should be either pure white flesh or have a soft pink hue.

Lion Brand
EXTRA SUPER QUALITY
PIN KIEW GLUTINOUS RICE
PRODUCT OF THAILAND
NET WT. 1 KG.
A A A
Hung Cheong Company
SALTED RADISH
WAKAME
Dried Shrimp
Jelly Fish Strip
海蜇絲
Net Weight 500g
臘腸
Chinese Style
Lup Chong
175g NET
陽江豆豉
SALTED BLACK BEAN
100% NATURAL
Golden Sugar
CRYSTAL SUGAR
EXCELLENT PRODUCTS
黄冰糖
HENG FAI BRAND
All Natural And Healthy
しいたけ
HENG FAI TRADING CO. PTY. LTD.
Vermicelli
BEAN THREAD
特級粉絲
100g
腐皮
Best Before
P.Code: DBSK2

WAH KEE
辣椒油
CHILLI OIL
特級花雕酒
CHINESE COOKING WINE
特級花雕酒
CHINESE COOKING WINE
廚 640ml 用
成份:水,米,麥,焦糖色,鹽
Ingredients:water,rice,wheat,caramel,salt
Alcohol. 9.5%Vol Salt 1.5%
PRODUCT OF CHINA
金童牌正魚露
FISH SAUCE
GOLDEN BOY BRAND
SINCE 1914
HACCP
NET WT 725 mL (24 FL.OZ.)
POIDS NET 725 CC. (1PT. 8FL.OZ.)
Megachef
น้ำปลาแท้
PREMIUM FISH SAUCE
Traditionally prepared with
fresh anchovies and
pure sea salt

They should not be sitting on mounds of ice either, as ice burns the flesh, making it soggy. Fresh fish fillets will have a slightly oily look as well, pointing to the fact that they have not been under ice, kept in water or been frozen. If you wish, you can purchase a whole fish and ask the fishmonger to fillet it for you on the spot – this way, you'll know that the fillets will be in great shape.
see also Prawns

Fish sauce
This clear, amber-coloured liquid is the product of salted and fermented fish, and it has a unique, pungent taste and aroma. It is one of my favourite seasonings – I use it in stir-fries, marinades, braises, salad dressings and dipping sauces. Reliable brands include Megachef, Squid and Golden Boy.

Five-spice powder
A variable mixture of 5–7 spices – cinnamon, star anise, fennel seed, cloves, liquorice root, Sichuan peppercorns, ground ginger – make up this exotic mix that is used in marinades and braises. Buy ready-ground and, as with any dried spice, store in an airtight container away from light, heat and moisture.

Five-spice pressed tofu *see* **Tofu**

Garlic
This has been integral to the food and medicine of East Asia for thousands of years – in fact, East Asians boast the world's highest per-capita garlic consumption! I particularly love simple but scrumptious stir-fries of Chinese vegetables tossed with salt and lashings of garlic. Garlic should be used within an hour or less of being prepared, whether minced, diced or crushed. Never use bottled minced garlic (it is filled with preservatives and tastes dreadful) or dried, powdered garlic. Always purchase the firmest heads of garlic – firmness is an indication of freshness.

Garlic chives
Also known as Chinese chives, these look like a more robust version of regular chives, with flat, slender bright-green stems. They are sold in bunches, sometimes with edible flower buds, at Asian supermarkets and some greengrocers. Yellow garlic chives have slightly thinner leaves, but the same garlicky flavour.

Ginger
Fresh ginger, with its clean, aromatic flavour, is a mainstay of Chinese cuisine – especially in combination with spring onions and soy sauce. Always choose the firmest, heaviest roots with smooth, taut skin and avoid any wrinkled-looking pieces, as they will be dry and fibrous in texture and weak in taste. Look out for young ginger when it is in season, from late summer to early autumn: it is pale yellow, with pink stems and fine skin (there's no need to peel it), and is incredibly tender and delicately flavoured.

Glass (bean thread) noodles
Also known as cellophane noodles, these transparent vermicelli-like noodles are made from ground mung beans, and are usually sold dried and tied in small bundles. They need to be soaked in hot water for 15 minutes and drained before use.

Grapeseed oil
This light, clean-tasting oil is perfect for salad dressings.

Hokkien noodles
Everybody loves Hokkien noodles: they are robust, inexpensive, readily available, comforting and easy to cook. When buying them, always check the use-by date and avoid any that seem slimy or have greenish tinges. Try to find ones made with fresh eggs rather than yellow food colouring (if in doubt, check the ingredients listing).

King brown mushrooms
A species of oyster mushroom, king brown mushrooms are now cultivated in Australia and are becoming increasingly available. Perfect for stir-frying, they have dense flesh and a thick but tender beige stem that is as flavoursome as the cap, with a strong, rich and meaty flavour.

Lotus root
Actually a rhizome, lotus 'root' is ivory-coloured, with swellings along its length similar to sausage links and a beautiful honeycomb pattern when cut crossways. As it is grown in ponds, it requires thorough washing to remove any muddy residue. Fresh lotus root is seasonally available in Chinese supermarkets; at other times, look for frozen sliced lotus root.

Lup cheong sausage
With its chewy texture and salty flavour, this more-ish and delicious dried pork sausage lends a unique colour, sweetness and richness to a dish. It is widely available in supermarkets and Asian grocers.

Malt vinegar
I like the slightly caramelly flavour and golden colour of this vinegar, which is brewed from barley and wheat.

Meat and poultry
When purchasing meat or poultry, I strongly recommend that wherever possible you buy chemical-and hormone-free, non-genetically-modified, free-range and organically raised. Not only is the taste sweeter, more refined and clean, the texture more tender and the nutrient and mineral content much higher; but also filling meat and poultry with hormones, preservatives and chemicals is simply unfair to the animal, and ingesting it is detrimental to our overall health.

Miso paste
This is made from soybeans, a grain such as rice or barley, koji culture and a little salt, which are naturally fermented together. The grain used and the fermentation process determine the characteristics of the miso – the longer the fermentation time, the darker the colour. Traditionally, darker red or brown miso is eaten in the cooler months, and the lighter white miso in the summer months. Miso is available in most supermarkets, but you'll find the widest range in Asian supermarkets and health-food shops.

Mushrooms *see* Black cloud ear fungus; Dried Chinese mushrooms; Enoki mushrooms; King brown mushrooms; Oyster mushrooms; Shiitake mushrooms; Shimeji mushrooms; Swiss brown mushrooms

Noodles *see* Glass (bean thread) noodles; Hokkien noodles; Rice noodle sheets; Rice vermicelli; Thin egg noodles

Nutmeg
This sweet, aromatic spice appears in the regional cuisine of northern China and Inner Mongolia, where Middle Eastern flavourings have been incorporated into the food culture. It is mostly used in rich, meaty braises.

Oyster mushrooms
These cream-coloured, fan-shaped mushrooms have been cultivated in Asia for years, and are now grown in Australia. Named for their subtle taste of the sea, they have a rich, velvety texture and are at their best stir-fried, braised or steamed. They are available in most supermarkets.

Peanut oil
Because it can be heated to high temperatures without burning, peanut oil is perfect for stir-frying, deep-frying and scalding. The nutty, toasty, smoky flavour that heated peanut oil imparts to a dish means that it is a must-have in the Chinese pantry. However, if you are allergic to peanuts, vegetable oil with a dash of sesame oil makes a good substitute.

Prawns
When purchasing prawns, look for a firm texture and vibrant appearance. Unlike fish, prawns store well in an ice slurry (ice and water), but frozen prawns – like any frozen seafood – are tasteless, lacking their naturally sweet and salty oceanic flavour. I find ready-cooked prawns are often overdone, so I prefer to buy uncooked ('green') prawns and poach or steam them myself for no longer than 3–4 minutes.

Preserved mustard greens
These are the stems and leaves of fresh mustard greens pickled in sugar, salt and vinegar. Used sparingly, they have a pungent, salty taste and a wonderful crunchy texture. Available from Asian supermarkets.

Red shallots
These small pink shallots have a more refined and delicate taste than either golden shallots or onions. Available from Asian grocers and some supermarkets.

Rice
To the Chinese, eating rice is synonymous with eating a meal, and they feel they haven't truly eaten unless they have had rice. I mostly use medium-grain or jasmine rice – except when making sticky rice parcels, where the shorter, plumper grains of glutinous rice give a lovely chewy texture. Jasmine rice and medium-grain rice are widely available, but you may need to go to an Asian grocer for glutinous rice.

Rice noodle sheets
These large, thin sheets of noodles are made from rice, water, starch and peanut oil, and have a delicious silky, slippery texture. They are brilliant for stir-frying, steaming and adding to soups. Dick Ap is my preferred brand, but there are plenty of others to choose from.

Rice vermicelli
Made from rice flour, these very fine off-white noodles are sold dried in skeins, and need to be soaked in hot water for about 10 minutes and drained well before being used in soups, salads and stir-fries. They're available in most supermarkets – I like Wai Wai brand.

Salad vegetables and herbs
When I use lettuces and herbs in my Chinese cooking, I mostly use them raw, so freshness is vital. Take time to touch, look and smell the various bunches on the refrigerated shelves – don't be embarrassed if you are seen foraging for the fresher bunch at the back! After all, there is nothing wrong with demanding fresh, quality produce. Look for intensely coloured salad vegetables and herbs, and check for brown-tinged slimy leaves or any signs of caterpillar infestation. Again, wherever and whenever possible, I urge you to buy chemical- and pesticide-free produce. Because the flavour of such produce is much more intense, you only need to purchase small amounts . . . what counts is quality, not quantity.

Salt flakes
Salt brings out the natural flavours in food and also draws out its moisture. I use salt flakes for their purity and natural flavour, as well as their flaky texture. Many table and kitchen salts are over-refined and adulterated with anti-caking agents and the like, but I think it's important to use good-quality salt – try to find Maldon or Murray River salt flakes.

Salted black beans
Also known as fermented black beans, these small soy beans are preserved by fermentation with salt and spices, which gives them their distinctively salty, rich taste and pungent smell. They are frequently used in conjunction with ginger and garlic and have a particular affinity with seafood and rich meats. Some people insist on rinsing black beans before use, but I never do. Double Rings is a good brand.

Made in Australia. Certified Organic
hulledorganictahini
this earth
this food. net 375g
SHOYU
SPIRAL
organic
250ml
TAMARI
SPIRAL
organic
Wheat Free
Natural
Soy Sauce
500ml
Ingredients:
Organic soybeans,
water, grain alcohol
and sea salt.
MUSO
UNPASTEURIZED
CERTIFIED ORGANIC
BROWN RICE MISO
味噌
Net Wt. 400g
spiral
miso
Miso (soybean paste)
is a product of natural
fermentation of whole
soybeans and grain.
Use freely in soups,
stews, sauces, spreads
and all styles
of cooking.
400g
BROWN
GENMAI
RICE
VINEGAR
SPIRAL
organic
250ml

CORNWELL'S
WHITE
VINEGAR
Free from artificial colours, flavours and preservatives
750 mL
CORNWELL'S
MALT
VINEGAR
750 mL
1kg
AUSTRALIA'S FAVOURITE
CSR
dark
BROWN SUGAR
100% natural
CHANG'S
PURE
SESAME
Oil
DELICIOUS AROMATIC OIL
280mL
KIKKOMAN
NATURALLY BREWED
Soy Sauce
ALL-PURPOSE
CSR
brown
SUGAR
500g
McWI

Salted jellyfish
The Chinese love jellyfish for its wonderfully unusual, crunchy yet gelatinous texture that's perhaps best described as tender rubber bands. Sold at Chinese grocers, salted jellyfish needs to be soaked in cold water for at least an hour before use – it's great in salads, especially with a sharp, vinegary dressing.

Salted radish
This is white radish (daikon) that has been preserved in salt and sugar. Available whole, sliced or shredded in Asian grocery stores, it has a wonderful crunchy texture and an intensely salty taste.

Sesame oil
This amber-coloured oil is pressed from roasted sesame seeds. Used in small quantities so as not to overwhelm the subtleties of a dish, sesame oil adds an aromatic, nutty taste that enhances other flavours. Kinlan, Yeo's, Dynasty and Kodaya are all reliable brands.

Sesame paste
This is made from sesame seeds, which are ground to create a smooth paste similar to unhulled tahini (which can be used in its place). Sesame paste makes a beautiful base for sauces, creating a rich, smooth velvety texture, with a lovely nutty flavour.

Sesame seeds
Both white and black sesame seeds are a common garnish in Chinese cuisine, prized for their colour, taste and crunch. They should be dry-roasted before use to bring out their flavour. White sesame seeds are widely available, but you may need to seek out an Asian grocer or a specialist spice supplier for black sesame seeds.

Shao hsing wine
This is the staple cooking wine in China, where it has been made in the south-western province of Zheijiang for over 2000 years. Fermented from a blend of glutinous rice, rice millet, yeast and water, it is aged in earthenware vessels for about 10 years in underground cellars. Its rich, mellow taste enhances stir-fries, braises and stocks; like any alcohol, shao hsing deepens, broadens, sweetens and softens dishes, adding complexity of flavour. My favourite brand is Pagoda Blue Label Shao Hsing Huia Tiao Chew Brand, but dry sherry can also be used (see below).

Sherry
Like many traditional Chinese cooks, my mother uses dry sherry instead of shao hsing wine (see above); it has similar properties and makes a fine substitute.

Shiitake mushrooms
These rich-flavoured mushrooms have brown, velvety caps and pale cream stems. The stems can be quite tough and so are generally discarded, although they can be used to add depth of flavour to stocks. Fresh shiitake mushrooms are increasingly available in supermarkets.
see also Dried Chinese mushrooms

Shimeji mushrooms
This Japanese variety of mushroom is now cultivated in Australia, and can be found in greengrocers and some supermarkets. Off-white to soft grey in colour, shimeji mushrooms grow in clumps and are delicate with a nutty flavour that works well in stir-fries. Trim off the base before using.

Shoyu *see* Soy sauce

Sichuan peppercorns
These hollow reddish-brown 'peppercorns' are actually the dried berries of the prickly ash tree. They are intensely aromatic with a charming woody fragrance, and should always be dry-roasted before use to bring out all their aromatic oils. When eaten they leave a pleasantly numbing, tingly sensation on your tongue, which some find addictive – I can't live without them!

Silken tofu *see* Tofu

Soy sauce
This naturally fermented product is made from roasted soybean meal and usually wheat and then aged for up to two years. Dark soy sauce is aged longer than light soy sauce and mixed with molasses, which gives it that dark, caramel colour. Light soy sauce is used in dressings, stir-fries, braises and steamed dishes while dark soy sauce is better for marinades, stocks and braises. Some inferior versions are full of chemicals, so make sure you buy naturally fermented soy sauce: reliable brands include Kikkoman, Pearl River Bridge and Healthy Boy Yellow Label for light soy sauce; and Pearl River Bridge or Pun Chun Premium dark soy sauces.

Japanese soy sauces include the delicate shoyu, which is used as a general seasoning, and tamari, which is slightly richer in flavour, and traditionally is only served with sushi and sashimi. Tamari is available in a wheat-free version, though, which makes it a great all-purpose option for those who are gluten-intolerant. I like to use Spiral brand organic shoyu and tamari.

Star anise
The hard, star-shaped, eight-pointed seed pod from a member of the magnolia family, star anise has an extremely robust, liquorice-like flavour and scent. It is used in traditional Chinese stocks and braises, usually with soy sauce and cinnamon, and is an essential ingredient in five-spice powder. Its pretty and unusual appearance makes it a beautiful garnish as well.

Sugar *see* Brown sugar; White sugar; Yellow rock sugar

Swiss brown mushrooms
With a more pronounced flavour and firmer texture than regular white mushrooms, these stand up well to stir-frying and braising. They're available at most supermarkets.

Tamari *see* Soy sauce

Thai basil
Available from Asian grocers, this is similar in appearance to Italian basil but with smaller green leaves, dark purple stalks and buds and white flowers. Sometimes called Asian basil, it has a strong anise flavour and aroma.

Thin egg noodles
Made with wheat flour and egg, these delicate noodles are often used in soups and salads. Fresh or dried versions are widely available in supermarkets and Asian grocers.

Tofu
Also known as bean cake, soybean cheese and bean curd, tofu is a protein-rich, low-fat food made from soy milk coagulated using natural gypsum or nigari (derived from seawater).

Tofu has a distinctive smooth, silky, velvety texture and a rather neutral, bland taste; like mushrooms, it is a wonderful vehicle for flavour. An excellent and very versatile food – especially for vegetarians – it can be steamed, braised, stir-fried or deep-fried, with different types of tofu being most suitable for the various cooking methods.

Silken tofu has a soft, velvety texture and is perfect for steaming or adding to soups, while firm tofu feels quite literally firm and stands up better to stir-frying, deep-frying and braising. Five spice pressed tofu is also a firm-textured tofu, but is golden-brown in colour from having been braised in dark soy sauce and spices; its rich flavour works well in salads with Asian herbs.

When buying fresh tofu, always check the use-by date. There is nothing worse than tofu that has gone off: it takes on a rather unpleasant odour, and sometimes a yellowy-green slime appears on the tofu. Another warning sign is a bloated packet that feels as though it is about to explode – this indicates that the tofu is fermenting.

My favourite brands are Soya King silken tofu and firm tofu, and Unigreen '5 Spice Bean Cake' pressed tofu.

Turmeric
Widely available, ground turmeric is made from the dried rhizome of the turmeric plant. Earthy and slightly medicinal-tasting, a little bit goes a long way.

Vegetable oil
Cottonseed, canola, soybean, safflower and sunflower oils are perfect for deep-frying as they have a neutral, unobtrusive flavour and odour.

Vegetables
When choosing vegetables, always go for the most firm-skinned and tender young ones that are vibrant-coloured, intense and fresh-smelling. Obviously, you should avoid any vegetables with signs of wilting or browning, and those that are caterpillar-affected, fibrous or gnarly. Even when buying unusual vegetables that you may be unfamiliar with, these simple rules apply.
see also Salad vegetables and herbs

Vietnamese mint
Also called laksa leaf, this herb has small spear-shaped leaves. Used mainly in Thai and Vietnamese cooking – and available from Asian grocers – it adds a wonderful spicy citrus taste and fragrance to soups and salads.

Vinegar *see* Apple cider vinegar; Brown rice vinegar; Malt vinegar; White vinegar

White glutinous rice *see* Rice

White peppercorns
I tend to use white peppercorns instead of black peppercorns because they are hotter and less aromatic than black. When garnishing dishes with ground white pepper, be sure to sprinkle over only a small pinch, as it can be overpowering.

White radish (daikon)
Available from Asian grocers and some supermarkets, this long radish resembles an overgrown carrot, but is white in colour. It has crisp flesh with a juicy, crunchy texture and a mildly pungent, mustard-like flavour – it's great for eating raw, pickling or braising.

White sugar
The Chinese use white sugar extensively in stir-fries and dipping sauces.

White vinegar
I use this vinegar to make pickles and sauces. Although it can be rather harsh, when simmered the flavour seems to lengthen out – and in these preparations a punchy, vinegary note is desirable.

Winter melon
Available from Asian grocers, winter melon is a little like cucumber, with a watery, cleansing flavour and texture. It has a hard, dark green skin and seeds, both of which must be removed before cooking in soups or braises.

Wonton wrappers
Usually about 8 cm square, these are available in the refrigerated sections of most supermarkets in 250 g packets. I think there is little difference between the various brands; I always buy the yellow wonton wrappers that are made from eggs, flour and water, but the white ones made from just flour and water are equally good. Always check the use-by date, and reject any wrappers with dark mouldy spots visible through the packaging!

Wonton wrappers are useful not only for making wontons, but are also great simply fried in a little bit of vegetable oil – they puff up like crisps and go beautifully with a bowl of Chinese-style pickles.

Yellow rock sugar
Also known as golden crystal rock sugar, this sugar comes in the form of large crystals, and is available in boxes at Asian supermarkets. Widely used in Chinese cuisine, this sugar adds a glossiness and sheen to braises, stocks and steamed dishes, without making them overly sweet.

Medium Grain
White Rice
Sun Rice
energy source
99% fat free
cholesterol free
gluten free
low salt
1 kg
For recipes go to
www.sunrice.com.au
CORNWELL'S
PREMIUM
APPLE CIDER
VINEGAR
Free from artificial colours, flavours and preservatives
750 mL
AZALEA
COOK BOOK OFFER
100% PURE
GRAPESEED OIL
NATURAL SOURCE of VITAMIN E
CHOLESTEROL FREE
CONTAINS ANTIOXIDANT
& PLANT STEROLS
High smoke point - Light flavour
Ideal for grill or barbeque
1Litre
Made with the goodness of over 1,500 peanuts
Crisco
The healthy oil expert
Peanut Oil
Good Source of Mono-unsaturates
Cholesterol Free
750mL
AYAM
AYAM

Marinex

STOCKS

CHINESE VEGETABLE STOCK

The essence of a good vegetable stock is to begin with the freshest, best-quality raw vegetables. I like to fry the vegetables first with salt, which helps to bring out their natural flavours.

2 tablespoons vegetable oil
2 red onions, finely sliced
8 cm × 5 cm knob (50 g) ginger, thickly sliced
10 garlic cloves, crushed
1 tablespoon salt flakes
3 carrots, thinly sliced
6 sticks celery, thinly sliced
10 spring onions, trimmed and halved
1 bunch coriander, stems and roots only, washed and finely chopped
6 litres cold water

Heat oil in a large stockpot over high heat. Add onion, ginger, garlic and salt and fry for 1–2 minutes. Add carrot, celery, spring onion and coriander, reduce heat to medium–high and fry, stirring often, for a further 5 minutes or until vegetables are lightly browned.

Add water to pot and bring to the boil. Reduce heat to a gentle simmer, skimming the surface with a ladle to remove any impurities. Simmer for 1 hour, skimming as required.

Strain stock through a fine sieve lined with muslin and cool. Store, covered, in the refrigerator for up to 3 days or in the freezer for 2–3 months.

Makes about 3.5 litres

Use in
• Wakame Seaweed and Tofu Soup (page 42)
• Asian Mushroom and Cucumber Soup (page 45)
• Vegetable Dumpling Soup (page 46)
• Winter Melon and Potato Soup (page 49)

RICH CHINESE CHICKEN STOCK

Because I use this stock primarily for soups, it needs to be luscious and rich, since it forms the core ingredient of the dish. Remember, your stock will only be as good as your chicken!

1 × 1.6 kg free-range chicken
10 spring onions, trimmed and halved
1 large red onion, roughly chopped
8 cm × 5 cm knob (50 g) ginger, thickly sliced
10 garlic cloves, crushed
4 litres cold water
pinch salt

Rinse chicken and trim away excess fat from inside and outside cavity. Cut chicken into 10 pieces and place in a large stockpot with remaining ingredients. Bring to the boil, then reduce the heat to a gentle simmer, skimming the surface with a ladle to remove any impurities. Simmer for 2 hours, skimming as required.

Remove chicken pieces from stock and discard. Strain stock through a fine sieve lined with muslin and cool. Store, covered, in the refrigerator for up to 3 days or in the freezer for 2–3 months.

Makes about 2.5 litres

Use in
- Chicken, Oyster Mushroom and Glass Noodle Soup (page 58)
- Chicken, Silken Tofu and Chinese Cabbage Soup (page 61)
- Scallop and Ginger Dumpling Soup (page 62)

CHINESE BEEF STOCK

I love the rich flavour and gelatinous quality of oxtail. This stock, which includes dry-roasted spices, is inspired by the Vietnamese tradition, with the caramelisation of the onions, ginger and garlic adding depth and colour. What's more, you can shred the meat from the oxtail after you've made the stock and use it in Oxtail Soup with Rice Noodles, Pickled Carrot and Radish (page 57) or to replace the brisket in Red-Braised Brisket with Cherry Tomato Salad (page 96).

1 kg oxtail pieces
1 tablespoon coriander seeds
1 tablespoon fennel seeds
1 tablespoon cumin seeds
1 tablespoon Sichuan peppercorns
2 star anise
2 cinnamon quills
2 tablespoons peanut oil
10 spring onions, trimmed and halved
1 large red onion, roughly chopped
80 g ginger, thickly sliced
10 garlic cloves, crushed
6 litres cold water
pinch salt

Place oxtail in a large stockpot, cover with cold water and bring to the boil. Simmer for 10 minutes, then rinse well and drain. This will remove any impurities from the meat. Clean stockpot, return oxtail to pot and set aside.

Meanwhile, place all of the spices in a heavy-based frying pan over medium heat and dry-roast, tossing regularly, for 1½–2 minutes or until fragrant and just beginning to smoke. Remove from pan and set aside.

Heat the oil in a hot wok until the surface seems to shimmer slightly. Add the spring onions, red onion, ginger and garlic and stir-fry for 4–6 minutes or until caramelised to a deep golden colour.

Tip vegetable mixture into stockpot with oxtail, add roasted spices and water and bring to the boil, then reduce the heat to a gentle simmer, skimming the surface with a ladle to remove any impurities. Simmer for 2–2½ hours or until meat is falling off the bone. Skim as required.

Remove oxtail from stock. Strain stock through a fine sieve lined with muslin and cool. Store, covered, in the refrigerator for up to 3 days or in the freezer for 2–3 months.

Makes about 3.5 litres

Use in • Oxtail Soup with Rice Noodles, Pickled Carrot and Radish (page 57)

CHINESE PORK STOCK

Always use the best-quality pork to ensure a clean, fresh result. This stock is incredibly light, with a subtle pork aroma and flavour.

1 kg pork ribs, ribs separated
10 spring onions, trimmed and halved
1 large red onion, roughly chopped
80 g ginger, thickly sliced
10 garlic cloves, crushed
pinch salt
6 litres cold water

Place pork ribs in a large stockpot, cover with cold water and bring to the boil. Simmer for 10 minutes, then rinse well and drain. This will remove any impurities from the meat.

Clean stockpot and return pork ribs to the pot, along with remaining ingredients. Bring to the boil, then reduce the heat to a gentle simmer, skimming the surface with a ladle to remove any impurities. Simmer for 2–2½ hours or until meat is falling off the bone. Skim as required.

Remove pork ribs from stock and discard. Strain stock through a fine sieve lined with muslin and cool. Store, covered, in the refrigerator for up to 3 days or in the freezer for 2–3 months.

Makes about 3.5 litres

Use in • Pork Ball and Glass Noodle Soup with Garlic Chives (page 53)

WHITE MASTER STOCK

The main flavourings in this classic Cantonese stock are salt and shao hsing wine, hence the generous amount of each. Perfect for poaching poultry especially, it is best made fresh each time. Note that this stock cannot be served as a simple soup – it is just too salty for that purpose.

4 spring onions, trimmed and halved
6 garlic cloves, crushed
100 g ginger, thickly sliced
3 tablespoons salt flakes
500 ml (2 cups) shao hsing wine or dry sherry
3 litres cold water

Place all ingredients in a large stockpot and bring to the boil. Reduce heat to a gentle simmer and cook for 10 minutes to allow the flavours to infuse.

Use as directed in recipe or cool and store in an airtight container in the refrigerator for up to 3 days.

Makes 3.5 litres

Use in
• Crispy-Skin Chicken with Spicy Salt and Lemon (page 70)
• Quail with Chilli–Soy Dipping Sauce and Pickled Cucumber (page 78)
• White-Cooked Pork Belly with Pickles and Blistered Chillies (page 108)

紹興廚酒

RED BRAISE MASTER STOCK

I never tire of making this stock. Visually, it is just so beautiful: earthy, rich, natural tones, and the wonderful textures and colours of all those raw ingredients. It always reminds me of a big gutsy red wine, with its spicy and aromatic overtones, deep hue and complex flavours. The addition of soy sauce is the reason this stock is called 'red' braising, since it literally gives any meat or poultry cooked in it a dark reddish tone. This is one of the most-used stocks in my kitchen – it is so versatile, as it freezes exceptionally well and ages gracefully (just like wine). Dried tangerine peel would traditionally be used in this stock, but I find it can be rather musty and prefer to use fresh peel. I do sometimes use mandarin, tangerine or tangelo peel in place of the orange peel, though.

4 spring onions, trimmed and halved
80 g ginger, thickly sliced
6 garlic cloves, crushed
4 strips (about 6 cm × 1 cm) orange peel, white pith removed
8 star anise
4 cinnamon quills
375 ml (1½ cups) light soy sauce
250 ml (1 cup) shao hsing wine
185 g (1 cup) lightly packed dark brown sugar
1 teaspoon sesame oil
3 litres cold water

Place all ingredients in a large stockpot and bring to the boil, stirring to dissolve sugar. Reduce heat to a gentle simmer and cook for 25 minutes to allow the flavours to infuse.

Use as directed in recipe or cool and store in an airtight container in the refrigerator for up to 3 days.

After cooking with the stock, you can strain it and freeze it indefinitely to use again. It will develop a stronger flavour over time.

Makes 3.5 litres

Use in
- Red-Braised Duck Breast with Pickled Mushrooms (page 87)
- Red-Braised Brisket with Cherry Tomato Salad (page 96)
- Crispy Orange-Peel Beef (page 100)
- Red-Braised Pork Belly with Eggs, Carrot and Shallots (page 115)
- Red-Braised Pork Belly with Green Chillies and Garlic (page 116)
- Salad of Caramelised Duck and Lychees (page 237)
- Salad of Red-Braised Poussin, Black Cloud Ear Fungus and Celery (page 238)

SOUPS

WAKAME SEAWEED AND TOFU SOUP

My first trip to Japan was life-changing; I was particularly fascinated by the way the Japanese use seaweed in their cooking. Wakame is exceptionally good for you, with its high mineral and nutrient content. I love the slippery, unusual texture of it and its refreshing, oceanic flavour. This is a very simple, light, healing type of soup, with its clean flavours and wholesome ingredients.

50 g dried wakame seaweed
70 g baby spinach
1 × 300 g packet silken tofu
1.5 litres Chinese Vegetable Stock (page 28)
5 cm × 2 cm knob (20 g) ginger, cut into fine julienne strips
2½ tablespoons light soy sauce
1 teaspoon salt flakes
1 teaspoon white sugar
½ teaspoon sesame oil
sliced red chillies in light soy sauce, to serve (optional)

Soak wakame in plenty of cold water for 10 minutes to rehydrate and soften. Drain well. (I like to use the nutrient-rich soaking water on my plants.) Using scissors, cut off the hard 'rib' from the wakame strips and discard, then cut each strip into rough pieces for ease of eating. Divide wakame and baby spinach among 4 bowls.

Gently remove tofu from packet and invert onto a plate. Carefully cut into 8 squares, then halve horizontally so you have 16 cubes. Set aside.

Place the vegetable stock, ginger, soy sauce, salt and sugar and sesame oil in a heavy-based saucepan and bring to the boil.

Reduce the heat to a simmer, carefully slide tofu into the boiling stock and cook for 2 minutes to warm the tofu through.

Gently scoop out tofu using a slotted spoon and place 4 cubes in each bowl, then ladle soup into bowls. Serve with a small bowl of chillies in soy sauce, if you like.

Serve as a starter for 4

ASIAN MUSHROOM AND CUCUMBER SOUP

There is such a great assortment of exotic Asian mushrooms available now. I love the rustic look of them, and I love the way they soak up flavours, just like a sponge. This is an excellent soup for vegetarians, and the addition of Thai basil gives it an unusual twist.

1.5 litres Chinese Vegetable Stock (page 28)
5 cm × 2 cm knob (20 g) ginger, cut into fine julienne strips
2½ tablespoons light soy sauce
1 teaspoon salt flakes
1 teaspoon white sugar
½ teaspoon sesame oil
100 g (1 packet) oyster mushrooms, torn
100 g (1 packet) enoki mushrooms, trimmed
100 g (1 packet) fresh black cloud ear fungus, cores removed, torn
1 small cucumber, peeled and cut into thin half-moons
1 bunch Thai basil, leaves picked
sliced red chillies in light soy sauce, to serve (optional)

Place vegetable stock, ginger, soy sauce, salt, sugar and sesame oil in a heavy-based saucepan and bring to the boil.

Add oyster and enoki mushrooms, reduce heat to a simmer and cook for 1 minute. Add black fungus and cucumber and simmer for a further 1 minute.

Ladle soup into 4 bowls and top with basil leaves. Serve with a small bowl of chillies in soy sauce, if you like.

Serve as a starter for 4

VEGETABLE DUMPLING SOUP

The vegetable dumplings are a little fiddly to make, yet their fresh flavours and slippery, comforting texture are absolutely worth the effort. The dumplings are definitely best made fresh on the day, but you could make the stock beforehand and freeze it, to give you a head start. This makes a hearty first course, or a complete meal in a bowl if you divide this amount between just 2 people.

---

16 Vegetable Dumplings (page 285)
1.5 litres Chinese Vegetable Stock (page 28)
5 cm × 2 cm knob ginger (20 g), cut into fine julienne strips
2½ tablespoons light soy sauce
1 teaspoon salt flakes
1 teaspoon white sugar
½ teaspoon sesame oil
2 spring onions, finely sliced
sliced red chillies in light soy sauce, to serve (optional)

Make the vegetable dumplings and set aside.

Place vegetable stock, ginger, soy sauce, salt, sugar and sesame oil in a heavy-based saucepan and bring to the boil.

Drop the dumplings into the boiling stock and cook for 2 minutes or until wrappers are transparent and cooked.

Remove dumplings with a slotted spoon and divide among 4 bowls, ladle in soup and garnish with spring onion. Serve with a small bowl of chillies in soy sauce, if you like.

Serve as a starter for 4

WINTER MELON AND POTATO SOUP

Available from Asian grocers, winter melon is a little like cucumber, with a cleansing taste and a watery texture – in fact, if you cannot find it, cucumber can be substituted (for this recipe, use 4 small peeled cucumbers). The potatoes add heartiness to the soup, and the deep-fried thin garlic slices add a delicate texture as well as flavour.

- **2 potatoes (400 g), peeled**
- **500 g winter melon (about ¼ small one)**
- **1.5 litres Chinese Vegetable Stock (page 28)**
- **5 cm × 2 cm knob (20 g) ginger, cut into fine julienne strips**
- **2½ tablespoons light soy sauce**
- **1 teaspoon salt flakes**
- **1 teaspoon white sugar**
- **½ teaspoon sesame oil**
- **2 spring onions, finely sliced**
- **Deep-Fried Garlic Slices (page 219), to serve**
- **sliced red chillies in light soy sauce, to serve (optional)**

Cut potatoes into 1 cm cubes. Cut skin off winter melon, remove seeds, then cut flesh into 1 cm cubes.

Place vegetable stock, ginger, soy sauce, salt, sugar and sesame oil in a heavy-based saucepan and bring to the boil.

Add potatoes and cook for 5 minutes, then add winter melon and cook for a further 5 minutes or until both vegetables are tender.

Ladle soup into 4 bowls and top with spring onion. Garnish with deep-fried garlic slices and serve with a small bowl of chillies in soy sauce, if you like.

Serve as a starter for 4

PORK AND WATER-CRESS SOUP WITH PICKLED WHITE ONION

The piquant pickled onion balances out the pork's richness with a lovely acidity, and the fresh scent and aroma of watercress complements the soup as a whole.

2 Braised Chinese Mushrooms (page 220), stems discarded and caps finely sliced
5 cm × 2 cm knob (20 g) ginger, cut into fine julienne strips
2 tablespoons fish sauce
60 g (⅓ cup) lightly packed brown sugar
1 bunch watercress, sprigs picked and washed
pinch freshly ground white pepper
sliced red chillies in light soy sauce, to serve (optional)

SOUP BASE
500 g free-range boneless pork shoulder, skin on, cut into quarters
8 spring onions, trimmed and halved
1 small red onion, roughly chopped
6 cm × 5 cm knob (40 g) ginger, thickly sliced
5 garlic cloves, crushed
3 litres cold water

QUICK PICKLED WHITE ONION
1 small white onion, thinly sliced
1 teaspoon salt flakes
1 teaspoon white sugar
juice of 1 lemon

To make the soup base, place pork in a stockpot, cover with cold water and bring to the boil. Simmer for 10 minutes, then rinse well and drain. This will remove any impurities from the meat.

Clean stockpot and return pork to it, along with remaining ingredients. Bring to the boil, then reduce to a gentle simmer, skimming the surface with a ladle to remove any impurities. Simmer for 2–2½ hours or until pork is very tender and stock has reduced by half. Skim as required.

Meanwhile, to make the quick pickled white onion, place onion, salt and sugar in a bowl and combine well with your hands. Refrigerate for 30 minutes.

Remove pork from stock and cool a little. When cool enough to handle, pull meat apart into bite-sized pieces and set aside. Strain stock through a fine sieve lined with muslin into a clean saucepan. Add mushrooms, ginger and fish sauce and bring to the boil. Scoop out 80 ml (⅓ cup) stock and pour into a wok placed over high heat. Add brown sugar and stir to dissolve. Cook for 1½ minutes or until caramelised. The sauce will bubble up and become sticky. Add pork pieces and cook for 1 minute, tossing to coat well in the sauce.

Drain liquid from pickled onion well and squeeze with your hands to remove any excess liquid, then toss with lemon juice.

Divide sticky pork among 4 bowls. Ladle soup into bowls, top with watercress and pickled onion, and garnish with white pepper. Serve with a small bowl of chillies in soy sauce, if you like.

Serve as a starter for 4

PORK BALL AND GLASS NOODLE SOUP WITH GARLIC CHIVES

I always use minced pork belly for my pork balls as the layers of fat that run through the belly ensure tenderness and flavour. It is important to work the protein in the pork by slapping it against the side of a bowl – this action tenderises the meat. I like to add lots of herbs to the meat for a fresh, light, aromatic flavour, and then serve with a side plate of yet more fresh herbs – an idea inspired, of course, by the wonderful soups of Vietnam. Glass noodles add texture to the soup.

- 100 g glass (bean thread) noodles
- 1.5 litres Chinese Pork Stock (page 35)
- 5 cm × 2 cm knob (20 g) ginger, cut into fine julienne strips
- 2 tablespoons fish sauce
- 1 bunch garlic chives, cut into 7 cm lengths
- ¼ bunch dill, leaves picked
- ½ bunch coriander, leaves picked
- 1 bunch Thai basil, leaves picked
- sliced red chillies in light soy sauce, to serve (optional)

PORK BALLS

- 450 g minced pork belly
- 5 cm × 2 cm knob (20 g) ginger, finely diced
- 2 garlic cloves, finely diced
- 2 spring onions, finely sliced
- 1 large red shallot, finely chopped
- ¼ bunch dill, stems only, finely chopped
- ½ bunch coriander, stems and leaves finely chopped
- ½ bunch mint, leaves picked and roughly chopped
- 2 tablespoons light soy sauce
- 1 tablespoons shao hsing wine or dry sherry
- 1 teaspoon white sugar
- 1 teaspoon sesame oil
- 1 egg

Soak noodles in hot tap water for 15 minutes. Drain well.

For the pork balls, line a tray or large plate with baking paper. Take small handfuls of the minced pork and slap against the side of a large bowl in order to work the protein, which will tenderise the meat. Add remaining ingredients and mix thoroughly using your hands. Scoop up 1 tablespoon of pork mixture and roll gently between wet palms to form a ball. Place on the baking paper and repeat with remaining mixture to make 20 balls in total.

Place pork stock, ginger and fish sauce in a heavy-based saucepan and bring to the boil.

Add half the pork balls to the boiling stock and cook for 7–8 minutes or until cooked through. Scoop out using a slotted spoon and keep warm while you cook the rest. Divide pork balls among 4 bowls.

Add noodles to stock and cook for 30 seconds to warm through. Ladle soup and noodles into bowls and garnish with garlic chives. Serve with a side plate of herbs and a small bowl of chillies in soy sauce, if you like.

Serve as a starter for 4

BEEF, TOMATO AND LOTUS ROOT SOUP

I am always cooking with brisket – one of the lesser cuts of the beast, yet it is so flavoursome and interestingly textured. Lotus root is available in Chinese grocery stores; if you cannot find fresh, use frozen. This comes pre-cut into 5 mm slices, which need to be defrosted and patted dry with paper towel before being used in this recipe.

---

5 cm × 2 cm knob (20 g) ginger, cut into fine julienne strips
2 tablespoons fish sauce
1 teaspoon brown sugar
4 small iceberg lettuce leaves, torn
sliced red chillies in light soy sauce, to serve (optional)

SOUP BASE
500 g brisket, cut into quarters
2 teaspoons coriander seeds
2 teaspoons fennel seeds
2 teaspoons cumin seeds
2 teaspoons Sichuan peppercorns
1 star anise
1 cinnamon quill
1 tablespoon peanut oil
8 spring onions, trimmed and halved
1 small red onion, roughly chopped
6 cm × 5 cm knob (40 g) ginger, thickly sliced
5 garlic cloves, crushed
3 litres cold water

CARAMELISED LOTUS ROOT
1 tablespoon peanut oil
5 cm × 2 cm knob (20 g) ginger, cut into fine julienne strips
12 slices (220 g) lotus root, peeled and cut into 5 mm slices then halved
2 large ripe tomatoes, quartered
2 tablespoons shao hsing wine or dry sherry
2 tablespoons brown sugar
1 tablespoon fish sauce

To make the soup base, place brisket in a stockpot, cover with cold water and bring to the boil. Simmer for 10 minutes, then rinse well and drain. This will remove any impurities from the meat. Clean stockpot, return brisket to it and set aside.

Meanwhile, place all of the spices in a heavy-based frying pan over medium heat and dry-roast, tossing regularly, for 1½–2 minutes or until fragrant and just beginning to smoke. Remove from pan and set aside.

Heat the oil in a hot wok until the surface seems to shimmer slightly. Add spring onions, red onion, ginger and garlic and stir-fry for 4–6 minutes or until caramelised and deep golden. Tip contents of wok into stockpot with brisket, add roasted spices and water and bring to the boil, then reduce the heat to a gentle simmer, skimming the surface with a ladle to remove any impurities. Simmer for 2–2½ hours or until brisket is very tender and stock has reduced by half. Skim as required.

Remove brisket from stock and cool a little. When cool enough to handle, pull meat apart into bite-sized pieces, discarding fat, and set aside. Place stock, ginger, fish sauce and sugar in a large saucepan and bring to the boil.

Meanwhile, make the caramelised lotus root. Heat oil in a hot wok until the surface seems to shimmer slightly. Add ginger and lotus root and stir-fry for 1 minute, then add tomatoes and stir-fry for another minute. Next, add wine or sherry and cook for 1 minute. Add sugar and fish sauce and cook for 3 minutes or until lotus root is tender but still crunchy and sauce is sticky. Tip lotus root, tomatoes and sauce into boiling stock, add brisket and cook for 2 minutes to warm beef through. Remove from heat and add lettuce.

Ladle soup into bowls and serve – with a small bowl of chillies in soy sauce, if you like.

Serve as a starter for 4

OXTAIL SOUP WITH RICE NOODLES, PICKLED CARROT AND RADISH

There is nothing more delicious than fresh rice noodles that become silken and slippery as they slide through a hot broth. Because there are several steps to this Vietnamese-style soup, you might want to make the stock beforehand and freeze it until required. I like to serve each element separately, so you can enjoy the individual nature of each one, as well as the flavoursome stock, but you could just as easily combine everything in one bowl in the usual manner – either way, this is luscious.

---

500 g fresh rice noodle sheets
1.5 litres Chinese Beef Stock (page 32)
5 cm × 2 cm knob (20 g) ginger, cut into fine julienne strips
2 tablespoons fish sauce
1 teaspoon brown sugar
1 bunch mint, leaves picked
sliced red chillies in light soy sauce, to serve (optional)

QUICK PICKLED CARROT AND RADISH
1 small carrot, cut into fine julienne strips
150 g white radish (daikon), cut into fine julienne strips
1 teaspoon salt flakes
1 teaspoon white sugar
juice of ½ lemon
½ teaspoon fish sauce

CARAMELISED OXTAIL
oxtail meat from Chinese Beef Stock (page 32)
60 g (⅓ cup) lightly packed brown sugar
2 tablespoons fish sauce

To make the quick pickled carrot and radish, place carrot, radish, salt and sugar in a bowl and combine well with your hands. Refrigerate for 1–2 hours.

Cut block of rice noodle sheets into 5 mm ribbons and gently pull apart to separate.

Place stock, ginger, fish sauce and sugar in a large saucepan and bring to the boil.

Meanwhile, make the caramelised oxtail. Pull meat apart into bite-sized pieces (or, if you are like me and love to suck on the bones, leave as whole pieces). Scoop out 80 ml (⅓ cup) of stock from the pan and pour into a wok placed over high heat. Add sugar and stir to dissolve. Cook for 1½ minutes or until caramelised – the sauce will bubble up and become sticky. Add oxtail meat and fish sauce and cook for 1 minute, tossing to coat well in the sauce.

Drain liquid from pickled carrot and radish, squeeze with your hands to remove any excess liquid, then toss with lemon juice and fish sauce.

Add rice noodles to stock and cook for 1 minute to warm through noodles. Using tongs, divide noodles and sticky oxtail among 4 bowls, then top with pickled carrot and radish. Ladle stock into separate bowls and serve with mint leaves on the side – plus a small bowl of chillies in soy sauce, if you like.

Serve as a starter for 4

CHICKEN, OYSTER MUSHROOM AND GLASS NOODLE SOUP

For maximum flavour, I marinate the chicken first and then stir-fry it before adding it to the soup – and for maximum tenderness, I use chicken thigh fillets. Fresh coriander, bean sprouts, chilli and lemon juice are a great way to add another dimension to this soup.

---

100 g glass (bean thread) noodles
1.5 litres Rich Chinese Chicken Stock (page 31)
5 cm × 2 cm knob (20 g) ginger, cut into fine julienne strips
2 tablespoons fish sauce
1 tablespoon peanut oil
100 g oyster mushrooms, torn
2 spring onions, cut into fine julienne strips
Deep-Fried Garlic Slices (page 219)
180 g (2 cups) bean sprouts
½ bunch coriander, leaves picked
1 lemon, cut into quarters

MARINATED CHICKEN
400 g free-range chicken thigh fillets (about 2 small ones), cut widthways into 1 cm thick slices
5 cm × 2 cm knob (20 g) ginger, finely diced
1 garlic clove, finely chopped
1¼ tablespoons light soy sauce
1 tablespoon shao hsing wine or dry sherry
2 teaspoons white sugar
½ teaspoon sesame oil

To make the marinated chicken, place all ingredients in a bowl and mix well. Refrigerate for 1 hour.

Soak noodles in hot tap water for 15 minutes. Drain well.

Place chicken stock, ginger and fish sauce in a heavy-based saucepan and bring to the boil.

Meanwhile, heat peanut oil in a hot wok until the surface seems to shimmer slightly. Add the marinated chicken and stir-fry for 2 minutes or until three-quarters cooked.

Transfer chicken to the boiling stock, add noodles and mushrooms and cook for 30 seconds.

Remove from the heat, add spring onions and ladle soup into 4 bowls. Garnish with deep-fried garlic slices, bean sprouts and coriander. Serve with lemon quarters on the side – and a small bowl of chillies in soy sauce, if you like.

Serve as a starter for 4

CHICKEN, SILKEN TOFU AND CHINESE CABBAGE SOUP

A very gentle, nurturing Cantonese-style soup, this makes the most of the wonderful contrasting textures of velvety silken tofu, crunchy Chinese cabbage and a little kick of pickled shallots.

- 1 × 300 g packet silken tofu
- 1.5 litres Rich Chinese Chicken Stock (page 31)
- 5 cm × 2 cm knob (20 g) ginger, cut into fine julienne strips
- 1½ tablespoons light soy sauce
- 1 teaspoon salt flakes
- 1 teaspoon white sugar
- ½ teaspoon sesame oil
- 400 g free-range chicken breast fillet, cut widthways into 1 cm slices
- 1 bunch garlic chives, cut into 7 cm lengths
- 4 Chinese cabbage leaves, finely shredded
- sliced green chillies in light soy sauce, to serve (optional)

QUICK PICKLED RED SHALLOTS

- 2 red shallots, finely sliced
- ½ teaspoon salt flakes
- ½ teaspoon white sugar
- juice of ½ lemon

To make the quick pickled red shallots, place shallot, salt and sugar in a bowl and combine well with your hands. Refrigerate for 30 minutes.

Gently remove tofu from packet and invert onto a plate. Carefully cut into 8 squares, then halve horizontally so you have 16 cubes. Set aside.

Place chicken stock, ginger, soy sauce, salt, sugar and sesame oil in a heavy-based saucepan and bring to the boil. Add chicken and cook for 2 minutes or until cooked through. Scoop out chicken and divide among 4 bowls.

Reduce the heat to a simmer, carefully slide tofu into the boiling stock, along with the garlic chives, and cook for 2 minutes to warm the tofu through.

Meanwhile, drain liquid from pickled shallots, squeezing with your hands to remove any excess liquid, then toss with lemon juice.

Divide cabbage among bowls. Gently scoop out tofu and place 4 cubes in each bowl, then ladle soup into bowls. Garnish with pickled shallots and serve – with a small bowl of chillies in soy sauce, if you like.

Serve as a starter for 4

SCALLOP AND GINGER DUMPLING SOUP

Try and buy the freshest scallops you can find for these dumplings – steer well clear of frozen scallop meat, as it is flavourless and watery. If you're having trouble finding good scallops, you could always use fresh prawn meat or crabmeat instead. Because this soup is simply the dumplings and the stock, I think it's important to go all out on your stock and use rich Chinese chicken stock. I add shredded iceberg just before serving for a little crunch.

- **16 Scallop and Ginger Dumplings (page 282)**
- **1.5 litres Rich Chinese Chicken Stock (page 31)**
- **5 cm × 2 cm knob (20 g) ginger, cut into fine julienne strips**
- **1½ tablespoons light soy sauce**
- **1 teaspoon salt flakes**
- **1 teaspoon white sugar**
- **½ teaspoon sesame oil**
- **2 iceberg lettuce leaves, finely shredded**
- **sliced red chillies in light soy sauce, to serve (optional)**

Make the dumplings and set aside.

Place chicken stock, ginger, soy sauce, salt, sugar and sesame oil in a heavy-based saucepan and bring to the boil.

Drop dumplings into the boiling stock and cook for 2 minutes or until wrappers are transparent and filling is just cooked. To test if the dumplings are ready, remove one and cut into it with a sharp knife to see if the filling is hot.

Remove dumplings with a slotted spoon and divide among 4 bowls, ladle in soup and top with lettuce. Serve with a small bowl of chillies in soy sauce, if you like.

Serve as a starter for 4

POULTRY

BRAISED CHICKEN DRUMSTICKS WITH BLACK BEAN AND CHILLI

For me, chicken drumsticks are total comfort food – so affordable and accessible, especially now that free-range chicken is more widely available. Tossing the drumsticks in flour gives them a lovely rich coating, and also thickens the sauce. Black bean and chilli sauce is an all-time favourite (if you're cooking for children, you can easily omit the chilli) and goes beautifully with a range of ingredients. This dish is a great meal-in-one, served with steamed rice and Chinese greens.

- 3 tablespoons peanut oil
- 8 free-range chicken drumsticks
- 75 g (½ cup) plain flour
- 250 ml (1 cup) chicken stock or water
- ½ red capsicum (pepper), seeds removed, finely sliced
- 1 teaspoon malt vinegar

BLACK BEAN AND CHILLI SAUCE

- 1 tablespoon light soy sauce
- 1 tablespoon brown sugar
- 1 tablespoon malt vinegar
- 1 teaspoon sesame oil
- 2 tablespoons peanut oil
- 2 large red chillies, halved and seeds removed
- 2 large green chillies, halved and seeds removed
- 1 small red onion, finely sliced
- 5 cm × 2 cm knob (20 g) ginger, finely sliced
- 4 garlic cloves, crushed
- 1 large red chilli, finely sliced on the diagonal
- 2 tablespoons salted black beans
- 80 ml (⅓ cup) shao hsing wine or dry sherry

Heat half of the peanut oil in a hot wok until the surface seems to shimmer slightly. Toss drumsticks in flour to coat, shaking off any excess. Add half the drumsticks to the hot oil and sear for 1 minute each side. Remove drumsticks and drain on kitchen paper. Discard oil and wipe wok clean. Repeat with remaining oil and drumsticks, then wipe wok clean again.

To make the black bean and chilli sauce, combine soy sauce, sugar, vinegar and sesame oil in a small bowl and set aside. Heat peanut oil in a hot wok until the surface seems to shimmer slightly. Add halved chillies and cook for 30 seconds each side to blister and slightly blacken. Remove with tongs and drain on kitchen paper. Reserve oil in wok. Add onion, ginger, garlic, sliced chilli and black beans to hot oil in wok and stir-fry for 2 minutes, stirring regularly to make sure the black beans don't burn otherwise they will be bitter. Add wine or sherry and cook for 1 minute. Add soy sauce mixture to wok and stir-fry for 30 seconds.

Return drumsticks to wok and toss to coat in sauce for 1 minute. Add stock or water, cover with a lid, bring to the boil, then immediately reduce heat to a gentle simmer. Braise the chicken for 15 minutes or until cooked through. Remove from the heat, then add capsicum and vinegar to wok and toss to combine. Serve immediately, garnished with blistered chillies.

Serve as part of a banquet for 4

STIR-FRIED CHICKEN WITH TEA-SMOKED OYSTERS AND PICKLED CHILLIES

This is a variation on a classic Sichuanese-style dish of stir-fried chicken with pickled chillies and Sichuan pepper, to which I have added some wonderfully seductive tea-smoked oysters. You experience the taste sensations of spicy, smoky, piquant, salty and sour in every mouthful, all set against the tender, smooth texture of the chicken. With its complex flavours and intriguing textures, this dish is well worth the effort.

1¼ tablespoons light soy sauce
2 teaspoons brown sugar
1 teaspoon malt vinegar
½ teaspoon sesame oil
1¼ tablespoons peanut oil
500 g free-range chicken thigh fillets, cut into 1 cm thick slices
5 cm × 2 cm knob (20 g) ginger, cut into fine julienne strips
2 garlic cloves, roughly diced
2 tablespoons shao hsing wine or dry sherry
½ bunch garlic chives, cut into 7 cm lengths
12 Tea-Smoked Oysters (page 132), at room temperature
pinch Sichuan Pepper and Salt (page 306)
1 each red and green Pickled Chillies (page 257), finely sliced (optional)

Combine soy sauce, sugar, vinegar and sesame oil in a small bowl and set aside.

Heat 1 tablespoon peanut oil in a hot wok until the surface seems to shimmer slightly. Add half of the chicken and cook for 30 seconds each side to sear. Remove with a slotted spoon, then repeat with remaining chicken. Set chicken aside.

Add remaining peanut oil to wok. Add ginger and garlic and stir-fry for 10 seconds, then pour in wine or sherry and cook for 20 seconds, scraping base of wok to remove crisp bits.

Return chicken to wok, along with soy sauce mixture, and stir-fry for 1 minute or until chicken is just tender. Add garlic chives and toss to combine.

Transfer to a serving plate and spoon over sauce. Arrange oysters on top, then garnish with Sichuan pepper and salt – and pickled chillies, if desired. Serve immediately.

Serve as part of a banquet for 4–6

CRISPY-SKIN CHICKEN WITH SPICY SALT AND LEMON

The secret to crispy chicken skin lies in getting it super-dry before deep-frying the chicken. To ensure this, poach the chicken the day before and sit it on a rack set over a plate in your refrigerator overnight. If you don't want to serve the chicken chopped up Chinese-style, you could always serve it carved Western-style.

---

7 litres White Master Stock (page 36)
1 × 1.6 kg free-range chicken
vegetable oil, for deep-frying
2 tablespoons Spicy Salt (page 305)
lemon wedges, to serve
1 bunch coriander, sprigs picked

Make the white master stock in a stockpot large enough to hold the chicken comfortably.

Rinse chicken under cold water. Trim away excess fat from inside and outside the cavity, but keep neck, parson's nose and winglets intact.

When master stock is ready, return it to the boil. Lower chicken, breast-side down, into stock, ensuring it is fully submerged – you may need to weight it down with a plate – and poach chicken for exactly 14 minutes. There should be no more than an occasional ripple breaking the surface; adjust the temperature, if necessary. Do not put a lid on the pot at any stage.

Immediately remove pot from the heat and allow chicken to steep in the stock for 3 hours at room temperature to complete the cooking process. Using tongs, gently remove chicken from stock, being careful not to tear the breast skin. Place chicken on a tray or large plate and allow to cool.

Place chicken in fridge for a minimum of 3 hours, to allow the flesh to firm up and the skin to dry out. The drier the skin, the crispier it will become when deep-fried.

Place cooled chicken, breast-side up, on a chopping board. With a sharp knife or cleaver, make an incision along the centre of the breast. Using the heel of your hand, apply pressure to the top of your knife to chop through the breastbone. Use your hands and knife to ease apart the two halves of the chicken, then cut down one side of the backbone to separate them.

Pour enough oil to cover half of the chicken into a wok and heat until the surface seems to shimmer slightly (190°C). Carefully lower one chicken half into the hot oil so it is completely covered by the oil and deep-fry for 3 minutes each side or until the skin is golden brown and crisp. Carefully remove chicken with tongs and drain well on kitchen paper. Repeat with the other chicken half.

Once the chicken halves are cool enough to handle, chop them up Chinese-style (page 72), arrange on a platter and serve with a side dish of spicy salt, lemon wedges and coriander.

Serve as part of a banquet for 4–6

CHOPPING POULTRY CHINESE-STYLE

❶ Place cooked chicken (or duck) on chopping board, breast-side up.

❷ With a sharp knife or cleaver, cut along the centre of the breast. Using the heel of your hand, apply pressure to the top of your knife or cleaver to chop through the breast bone. Ease apart the two halves of the chicken.

❺ Cut bony pieces from the breast and discard.

❻ Chop each drumstick/thigh into slices about 5 cm x 2 cm and arrange on a platter.

❸ Cut off the wing from each breast and set aside.

❹ Make an incision between the drumstick/thigh and breast.

❼ Chop each breast across the bone into slices about 7 cm x 2 cm.

❽ Arrange breast slices on top of drumstick/thigh pieces.
Finally, cut each wing in half and lay on top of chicken.

CHINESE ROASTED CHICKEN

Most food cultures in the world have a recipe for roast chicken. This is one I have created based around the typical Chinese flavours of five-spice and ginger. First and foremost, use the best-quality chicken you can: free-range or organic, if possible. Rubbing the chicken inside and out with the five-spice and salt gives the chicken the most mouth-watering flavour. You can serve this either chopped Chinese-style or carved Western-style, with a fresh green salad.

1 × 1.6 kg free-range chicken
2 tablespoons salt flakes
½ teaspoon five-spice powder
4 garlic cloves, crushed
2 spring onions, halved
8 cm × 5 cm knob ginger (50 g), finely sliced
4 garlic cloves, finely sliced
2 teaspoons sesame oil
2 tablespoons light soy sauce

Preheat oven to 220°C. Rinse chicken under cold water. Trim away excess fat from inside and outside cavity, then trim off neck, parson's nose and winglets and discard. Pat chicken thoroughly dry with kitchen paper inside and out.

Combine 2 teaspoons salt with the five-spice powder and rub inside chicken cavity. Stuff cavity with the crushed garlic, spring onion and half of the ginger.

Gently loosen the skin from the chicken breast with your fingers, being careful not to tear it, then push the remaining ginger and the sliced garlic under the skin.

Rub the outside of the chicken with sesame oil and season with the remaining 1½ tablespoons salt. Place on a wire rack in a roasting tin and pour enough boiling water into the tin to reach a depth of 5 mm.

Roast for 15 minutes, then reduce oven temperature to 180°C and continue roasting for 35 minutes, adding more boiling water to the tin if it begins to dry out. To test if the chicken is ready, pierce the thigh with a skewer; if the juices run clear, the chicken is cooked.

Remove chicken from oven and allow to rest in the tin, uncovered, in a warm place for 15 minutes. Reserve cooking juices in tin.

When you're ready to serve, use a sharp knife or cleaver to cut the chicken in half through the breastbone. Transfer the garlic, spring onion and ginger from the cavity to a frying pan, along with any cooking juices from inside the bird. Add reserved juices from roasting tin, scraping any cooked-on bits from base of tin into pan. Place pan over high heat, add soy sauce and cook for 1 minute, just to heat through and reduce slightly. Pour into a small serving bowl.

Chop chicken Chinese-style (page 72) and arrange on a serving platter. Serve with the sauce on the side for dipping.

Serve as part of a banquet for 4

BRAISED CHICKEN WINGS WITH FRESH PINEAPPLE

This is an absolute all-time Kwong family favourite! Although I've been cooking this dish since I was about 10, my version has changed slightly over the years, and I now use beautiful organic chicken wings and fresh pineapple. This is perfect for dinner on a busy weeknight – the chicken wings are marinated (overnight is best, if this works for you), then simply braised and served with steamed rice.

12 free-range chicken wings (about 1.5 kg)
1 medium pineapple (about 900 g)
1 tablespoon peanut oil
1 white onion, cut into wedges
250 ml (1 cup) chicken stock or water
1 tablespoon light soy sauce, to serve

MARINADE

5 cm × 4 cm knob (30 g) ginger, cut into fine julienne strips
4 garlic cloves, crushed
80 ml (⅓ cup) shao hsing wine or dry sherry
3 tablespoons light soy sauce
1 tablespoon malt vinegar
1 tablespoon brown sugar
1 tablespoon cornflour
1 teaspoon sesame oil

Combine chicken wings with marinade ingredients in a large bowl. Cover and leave to marinate in the refrigerator for 1 hour, or overnight if possible.

Peel pineapple, cut in half and remove core. Slice pineapple into 5 cm × 1 cm pieces.

Heat oil in a large wok until the surface seems to shimmer slightly. Add onion and stir-fry for 1 minute. Add chicken wings and marinade and cook, turning occasionally, for 3 minutes or until lightly browned all over.

Add stock or water, cover with a lid, bring to the boil, then immediately reduce heat to a gentle simmer. Braise chicken wings for 10 minutes. Add pineapple and simmer for a further 10 minutes or until wings are cooked through.

Turn off the heat, then add soy sauce and toss to combine. Serve immediately.

Serve as part of a banquet for 4–6

QUAIL WITH CHILLI–SOY DIPPING SAUCE AND PICKLED CUCUMBER

This recipe is great for a cocktail party, where you just want some tasty and interesting little morsels. It also makes a great starter or light lunch. The pickles and chilli work well with the subtle flavours of the quail meat.

3.5 litres White Master Stock (page 36)
4 × 190 g quails, at room temperature
80 ml (⅓ cup) Chilli–Soy Dipping Sauce (page 301), to serve
60 g (½ cup) drained Pickled Cucumber (page 250), plus 1 tablespoon pickling liquid, to serve

Make the white master stock in a saucepan large enough to fit the quails snugly.

Rinse quails under cold water. Trim away excess fat from inside and outside cavity. Trim and discard neck, parson's nose and winglets.

When master stock is ready, return it to the boil. Lower quails, breast-side down, into stock, ensuring they are fully submerged – you may need to weight them down with a plate – and poach the birds gently for exactly 6 minutes. There should be no more than an occasional ripple breaking the surface; adjust the temperature, if necessary. Do not put a lid on the pan at any stage.

Immediately remove pan from the heat and allow birds to steep in the stock for 1 hour at room temperature to complete the cooking process.

Using tongs, gently remove birds from stock, being careful not to tear the breast skin, and place on a tray to drain. Reserve 3 tablespoons master stock and discard the rest.

Working with one quail at a time, place the bird breast-side up on a chopping board and halve lengthways, cutting through the backbone. Remove the internal organs and discard. Cut away the legs where they meet the body. Cut the backbone from the breast pieces and discard, then cut each breast in half so you have two pieces, one with the wing attached.

Arrange quail pieces on a platter and spoon over reserved master stock. Serve with side dishes of chilli-soy dipping sauce and pickled cucumber.

Serve as a starter for 4

CHICKEN AND BEAN CURD ROLLS

For me, this dish holds strong childhood memories of my mum's extraordinarily beautiful Chinese cooking. It is time consuming, but rewarding to make for dinner parties or cocktail parties. These rolls are very much about texture: the crackle of the papery bean curd skins and the salty crunch of the radish in the tender chicken filling. I add fresh dill to the filling for a wonderful fresh flavour, and sweet chilli sauce makes the perfect accompaniment.

4 sheets dried bean curd skin
80 ml (⅓ cup) vegetable oil
250 ml (1 cup) Sweet Chilli Sauce (page 297)
1 small cucumber, seeds removed, diced

CHICKEN FILLING
500 g chicken thigh fillet, coarsely minced
1 small carrot, cut into fine julienne strips
2 Braised Chinese Mushrooms (page 220), finely sliced
3 tablespoons salted radish, finely chopped
5 cm × 2 cm knob (20 g) ginger, finely diced
2 spring onions, finely sliced
½ bunch coriander, stems and roots only, washed and finely chopped
½ bunch dill, stems only, finely chopped
2 eggs
2 tablespoons shao hsing wine or dry sherry
2 tablespoons light soy sauce
1 tablespoon white sugar
1 tablespoon cornflour
1 teaspoon sesame oil

Place all chicken filling ingredients in a large bowl and mix well using your hands. Divide into 4 roughly equal portions.

Next, trim each bean curd skin into a 20 cm square. Cover the skins with a damp tea towel until needed to keep them malleable and stop them drying out.

To assemble, place a bean curd skin on a work surface, keeping the others covered. Scoop up a portion of the filling, place it near the bottom edge of the sheet then roll up the bean curd skin as tightly as possible. Dampen the edge with a little moisture from the filling and press firmly to seal. Leave the ends open and place the roll, seam-side down, on a plate that will fit inside a large steamer basket. Cover with a damp tea towel while you make the other rolls. Repeat this process with remaining wrappers and filling. Make sure the rolls are arranged in a single layer – use 2 plates if necessary.

Bring a large saucepan or wok of water to the boil.

Place plate inside steamer and cover with the lid. Position over the pan or wok of boiling water and steam the rolls for about 10–12 minutes or until cooked through. Using tongs and a spatula, carefully transfer the rolls to a chopping board, then cut each roll into 3 pieces and drain thoroughly on kitchen paper. Repeat with the remaining rolls if you used 2 plates to accommodate them.

Heat oil in a hot wok until the surface seems to shimmer slightly. Working in batches, carefully place the rolls in the wok and fry for about 1 minute each side or until golden brown. Carefully remove and drain well on kitchen paper.

To serve, combine the sweet chilli sauce and cucumber in a small bowl. Arrange the rolls on a platter and serve immediately with the dipping sauce.

Serve as a starter for 4–6 (makes 12 pieces)

CHICKEN WINGS STUFFED WITH PORK AND PRAWN

These delectable little mouthfuls of juicy chicken, stuffed with fresh prawn and pork, are something to make when you are relaxed and have plenty of time. De-boning the chicken wings is a bit fiddly and time-consuming, but the appearance and taste of the finished result makes it well worthwhile. I like to sear the stuffed chicken wings in oil just before serving them, to add another layer of texture.

---

12 free-range chicken wings (about 1.2 kg in total)
1 tablespoon peanut oil
½ bunch coriander, leaves picked (optional)
1 large red chilli, finely sliced

PORK AND PRAWN STUFFING
150 g pork belly, very finely chopped
400 g uncooked prawns, peeled, deveined and roughly chopped (about 160 g prawn meat)
5 cm × 2 cm knob (20 g) ginger, finely chopped
2 Braised Chinese Mushrooms (page 220), finely chopped
50 g salted radish, finely chopped
50 g preserved mustard greens, finely chopped
2 spring onions, finely sliced
2 tablespoons shao hsing wine or dry sherry
2 tablespoons light soy sauce
1 teaspoon white sugar
½ teaspoon sesame oil

First debone the chicken wings (page 84).

Bring a large saucepan or wok of water to the boil.

To make the pork and prawn stuffing, place pork in a large bowl. Take small handfuls of pork and slap against the side of the bowl in order to work the protein, which will tenderise the meat. Add remaining stuffing ingredients and mix thoroughly, using your hands.

Gently stuff each chicken wing with 1 tablespoon of filling and arrange them in a single layer on a plate that will fit inside a large steamer basket. Place plate inside steamer and cover with the lid. Position over the pan or wok of boiling water and steam for 15 minutes or until wings are cooked.

Carefully remove plate from steamer basket and, using tongs, place chicken wings on kitchen paper to drain. Reserve the cooking juices.

Heat oil in a hot wok until the surface seems to shimmer slightly. Add half of the chicken wings and sear for 45 seconds on each side, then remove and drain on kitchen paper. Repeat with the remaining chicken wings, then arrange on a serving platter. Spoon the reserved cooking juices around the chicken wings and garnish with coriander, if using, and chilli.

Serve as part of a banquet for 4–6 (makes 12)

DEBONING CHICKEN WINGS

❶ Place wing on chopping board and cut at the joint where it joins the drumette – it helps if you cut just below the joint.

❷ Cut off the wing tip.

❺ Make sure you have cut all the way to the wing-tip joint.

❻ Grab hold of the exposed bone and give it a good twist to pull it out.

❸ You can save the drumettes and wing tips to make stock, if you like.

❹ There are two bones in the wing that you need to remove. Using a sharp paring knife, and beginning with the smaller bone, run your knife along each side of the bone to cut the flesh away from the bone, trying not to tear the skin.

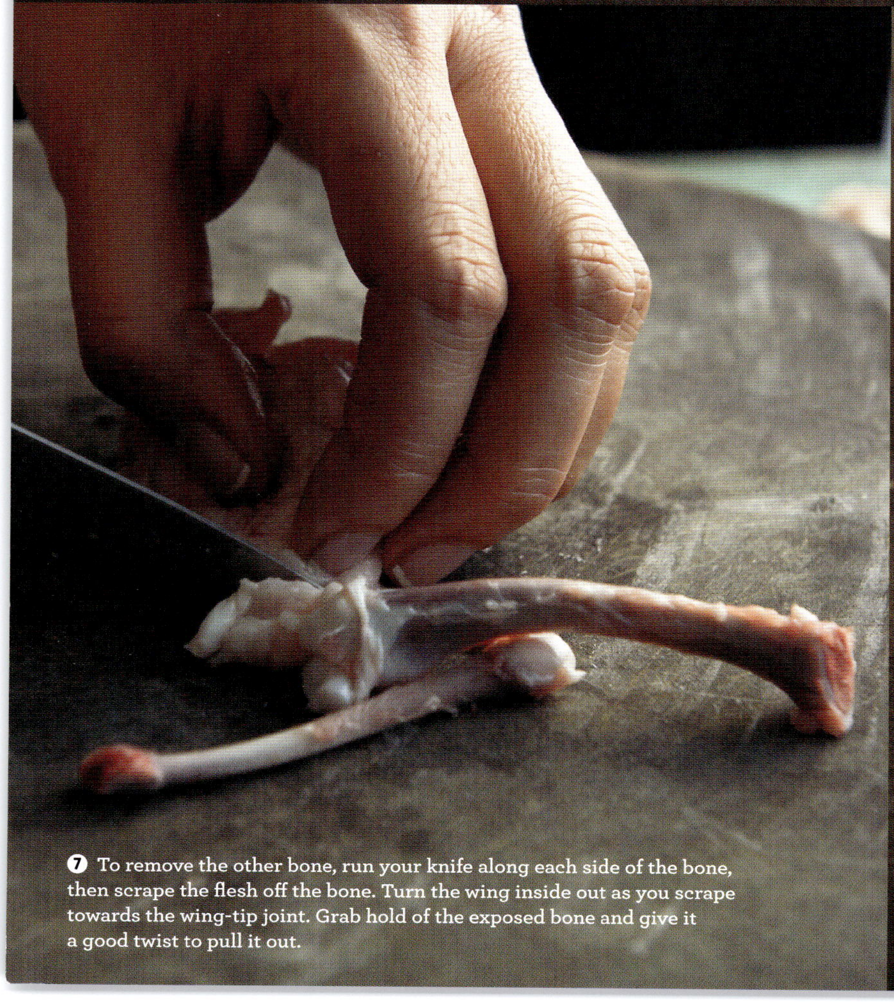

❼ To remove the other bone, run your knife along each side of the bone, then scrape the flesh off the bone. Turn the wing inside out as you scrape towards the wing-tip joint. Grab hold of the exposed bone and give it a good twist to pull it out.

❽ Repeat with the other chicken wings.

RED-BRAISED DUCK BREAST WITH PICKLED MUSHROOMS

A rather simple recipe, but with extremely impressive results. Duck breasts are readily available – and for those who don't have the wherewithal or desire to cook a whole duck, they are a great option. Because duck is naturally rich, I like to poach it in a robust, full-flavoured red braise master stock. It is important to allow the duck to steep in the stock for the time stated in the method, since this completes the cooking process. A very gentle way of cooking, this produces beautifully tender meat, and the pickled mushrooms provide an acidic note that cuts through the rich and juicy duck.

3.5 litres Red Braise Master Stock (page 39)
2 × 200 g free-range duck breasts, skin on, at room temperature
1 tablespoon dark brown sugar
1 teaspoon light soy sauce
1 teaspoon malt vinegar
¼ teaspoon sesame oil
125 g (½ cup) drained Pickled Mixed Mushrooms (page 258), to serve

---

Make the red braise master stock in a large saucepan.

When master stock is ready, return it to the boil. Lower duck breasts into the stock, ensuring they are fully submerged – you may need to weight them down with a plate – and poach duck for 5 minutes. There should be no more than an occasional ripple breaking the surface; adjust the temperature, if necessary. Do not put a lid on the pan at any stage.

Immediately remove pan from the heat and allow duck to steep in the stock for 2½–3 hours at room temperature to complete the cooking process.

When the duck is just about ready, make the sauce. Scoop out 250 ml (1 cup) master stock from the duck pan and place in a small saucepan. Add sugar, soy sauce, vinegar and sesame oil and cook over medium–high heat for 5 minutes or until reduced by half and syrupy.

Using tongs, gently remove duck breasts from stock and place on a tray or large plate to drain.

Cut duck breasts into 1 cm thick slices on the diagonal and arrange on a platter. Spoon over the sauce and serve at room temperature with pickled mushrooms.

Serve as a main course for 2 or as part of a banquet for 4

CHINESE ROASTED DUCK

I always prefer to roast a bird whole, whether it be duck, chicken, quail or poussin, as I find this results in more flavoursome and juicy meat. I love the rich texture and naturally salty flavour of miso and although it is traditionally used in Japanese cuisine, I tend to use it extensively in my Chinese kitchen. It is very good for you, with a lovely rich, dark colour and a paste-like texture that makes for a great marinade. For maximum flavour, it's important to rub the duck inside and out with the marinade. After cooking the duck, be sure to let it rest for the stipulated amount of time, to allow the flesh to relax and become tender.

---

1 × 2 kg free-range duck
8 cm × 5 cm knob (50 g) ginger, finely chopped
8 garlic cloves, finely chopped
2 tablespoons brown rice miso paste
2 tablespoons light soy sauce
2 teaspoons brown sugar
1 teaspoon chilli oil
2 spring onions, halved
3 star anise
2 cinnamon quills

Preheat oven to 200°C. Rinse duck under cold water. Trim away excess fat from inside and outside cavity, then trim off neck, parson's nose and winglets and discard. Pat duck thoroughly dry with kitchen paper inside and out.

Combine ginger, garlic, miso, soy sauce, sugar and chilli oil in a bowl and stir to dissolve miso and sugar. Rub all over duck and pour remaining mixture into duck cavity.

Place spring onion, star anise and cinnamon into the cavity. Place duck, breast-side up, on a wire rack in a roasting tin. Pour 250 ml (1 cup) water into the tin, then cover the entire tin with foil.

Roast for 35 minutes, then remove from oven. Increase oven temperature to 250°C. Remove foil and baste duck with cooking juices, then continue roasting, uncovered, for a further 15 minutes. To test if the duck is ready, pierce the thigh with a skewer; if the juices run clear, the duck is cooked.

Remove duck from oven and allow to rest in the tin, uncovered, in a warm place for 15 minutes.

To serve, tip cooking juices from duck cavity and roasting tin into a small bowl. Chop duck Chinese-style (page 72), arrange on a serving platter and pour over cooking juices.

Serve as part of a banquet for 4–6

MEAT

BEEF FILLET WITH ROASTED RICE AND PICKLED CHINESE MUSHROOMS

This is a flexible dish to have in your repertoire, as it can be prepared in stages over several days if that fits in more easily with your schedule. If possible, do try to marinate the beef overnight to obtain maximum flavour. The roasted rice adds both flavour and texture, offering a wonderful contrast to the silky meat; for maximum crunch, you really need to allow time for soaking the rice and letting it dry thoroughly, ideally overnight.

---

1 × 500 g piece best-quality beef fillet, cut into 3 equal pieces
1 tablespoon vegetable oil
1 lime, cut in half
6 Pickled Braised Chinese Mushrooms (page 253)

ROASTED RICE
65 g (⅓ cup) jasmine rice
1 heaped teaspoon Sichuan peppercorns

MARINADE
5 cm × 2 cm knob (20 g) ginger, finely diced
3 garlic cloves, finely diced
3 tablespoons shao hsing wine or dry sherry
2 tablespoons honey
2 tablespoons light soy sauce
½ teaspoon sesame oil

STICKY SAUCE
1 tablespoon light soy sauce
1 tablespoon brown sugar
1 teaspoon malt vinegar

To make the roasted rice, wash the rice well several times, then drain and place in a bowl. Add water to cover and soak for 2 hours. Drain the rice thoroughly, preferably overnight.

Combine beef with marinade ingredients in a bowl and toss to coat well. Refrigerate for at least 2 hours or overnight.

Place dried rice and Sichuan peppercorns in a frying pan over high heat and cook, stirring, for 7 minutes. First the rice will turn opaque, then a sandy colour, and the peppercorns will pop and release their fragrance. Transfer mixture to a shallow bowl and leave to cool to room temperature. Use a mortar and pestle or spice grinder to coarsely grind the rice mixture, then transfer to a glass jar and screw on the lid tightly to prevent any loss of fragrance.

Heat a barbecue or chargrill pan to high. Lightly brush grill or pan with vegetable oil. Remove beef from marinade, reserving the marinade, and grill beef for 4 minutes on one side. Turn over and grill for a further 2 minutes for medium-rare. Transfer beef to a plate and leave to rest in a warm place for 5 minutes.

Meanwhile, make the sticky sauce. Place the reserved marinade in a saucepan over medium–high heat. Add soy sauce, sugar and vinegar and bring to the boil, stirring to dissolve sugar. Cook for 4 minutes or until reduced by half and syrupy.

Cut beef into 5 mm thick slices and arrange on a platter. Sprinkle with 2 teaspoons roasted rice and serve with lime halves and a pile of pickled mushrooms on the side.

Serves as part of a banquet for 4–6

This recipe makes 45 g (⅓ cup) roasted rice. You will need only 2 teaspoons for this recipe, but the leftover rice will keep in an airtight container at room temperature for up to 2 months, and you can use it to add crunch to salads, noodles and so on. The Chinese braised mushrooms are heavenly when pickled in this way – their natural meatiness marries perfectly with the beef.

STIR-FRIED BEEF WITH KING BROWN MUSHROOMS AND GINGER

The better the quality of beef fillet you use for this dish, the better the end result will be. Organic, grass-fed beef has its own natural flavour and tenderness, and marinating it overnight really maximises these attributes. Stir-fried king brown mushrooms have a sublime, silky texture and an amazing ability to soak up flavours; their natural meaty quality works beautifully alongside the beef.

450 g beef fillet, cut into 8 mm thick slices
1 tablespoon light soy sauce
1 teaspoon sesame oil
1 teaspoon brown sugar
3 tablespoons peanut oil
5 cm × 4 cm knob (30 g) ginger, thinly sliced
3 garlic cloves, bruised
1 white or brown onion, cut into thin half-moons
150 g king brown mushrooms, cut into 5 mm thick slices
2 tablespoons shao hsing wine or dry sherry
2 spring onions, cut into 10 cm lengths

MARINADE
2 tablespoons shao hsing wine or dry sherry
1 tablespoon light soy sauce
1 teaspoon brown sugar
1 teaspoon malt vinegar
½ teaspoon sesame oil

Combine beef with marinade ingredients in a large bowl, cover, and leave to marinate in the refrigerator for at least 30 minutes or overnight.

Combine soy sauce, sesame oil and sugar in a bowl and stir to dissolve sugar.

Heat 2 tablespoons peanut oil in a hot wok until the surface seems to shimmer slightly. Add half the marinated beef and cook, without turning, for 30 seconds or until lightly browned. Turn over and cook the other side for 10 seconds. Remove from wok with a slotted spoon and keep warm. Repeat with remaining beef.

Wipe out wok. Heat remaining 1 tablespoon peanut oil in the hot wok until the surface seems to shimmer slightly. Add ginger, garlic and onion and stir-fry for 2 minutes or until onion is softened and caramelised.

Add mushrooms and stir-fry for 1 minute or until lightly coloured. Add wine or sherry and cook for 30 seconds. Add soy sauce mixture and stir-fry for 1 minute.

Return beef to wok, along with spring onion. Remove from the heat, then toss to combine and warm beef through. Serve immediately.

Serve as part of a banquet for 4

RED-BRAISED BRISKET WITH CHERRY TOMATO SALAD

A fresh, piquant and racy tomato salad balances the richness of this luscious braised brisket.

3.5 litres Red Braise Master Stock (page 39)
1 × 450 g piece beef brisket, halved

CHERRY TOMATO SALAD
12 cherry tomatoes, quartered
1 teaspoon white sugar
½ teaspoon salt flakes
½ bunch coriander, leaves picked
juice of 1 lemon
1 teaspoon fish sauce

Make the red braise master stock in a large saucepan.

Meanwhile, place brisket in a saucepan, cover with cold water and bring to the boil. Simmer for 10 minutes, then rinse well and drain. This will remove any impurities from the meat.

When the stock is ready, return it to the boil. Lower brisket into stock, ensuring it is fully submerged – you may need to weight it down with a plate – and poach brisket gently for 1½–2 hours or until the meat is very tender. There should be no more than an occasional ripple breaking the surface; adjust the temperature, if necessary. Do not put a lid on the pan at any stage. To check if it's ready, pierce the brisket with a small knife – you should meet no resistance.

About 15 minutes before you're ready to serve, make the cherry tomato salad. Combine tomato, sugar and salt in a bowl and refrigerate for 10 minutes.

Remove brisket from stock. Strain stock, discarding solids, and return to the heat.

When brisket is just cool enough to handle, pull apart into large bite-sized chunks and return to hot stock to gently warm through.

Take tomatoes from fridge, add coriander, lemon juice and fish sauce and toss to combine.

Remove brisket from stock using a slotted spoon and place on a serving plate. (Don't forget you can strain and freeze the master stock to use again.) Arrange cherry tomato salad on top of brisket and spoon over any juices from the bowl.

Serve as part of a banquet for 4

NORTHERN-STYLE BRAISED LAMB WITH SPICES

I am fascinated by the merging of Middle Eastern spices with traditional Chinese flavours that's found in northern China and Inner Mongolia. For this hearty dish I like to use dark brown sugar to make it extra rich and caramelly. If you want, you can also add other spices and aromatics, including cardamom, bay leaf or kaffir lime leaves. A squeeze of fresh lime juice at the end gives the whole dish a lift.

2 tablespoons peanut oil
8 cm × 5 cm knob (50 g) ginger, finely sliced
4 garlic cloves, crushed
1 small brown onion, halved and thickly sliced
600 g lamb shoulder meat, cut into 5 cm pieces
80 ml (⅓ cup) shao hsing wine or dry sherry
2 tablespoons dark brown sugar
2 tablespoons light soy sauce
2 large strips orange peel (about 8 cm × 3 cm), white pith removed
1 teaspoon malt vinegar
juice of ½ lime

SPICE MIXTURE
½ teaspoon ground turmeric
½ teaspoon ground coriander
½ teaspoon ground cumin
½ teaspoon ground nutmeg
½ teaspoon dried chilli flakes
1 cinnamon quill
2 star anise

Combine all spice mixture ingredients in a small bowl and set aside.

Heat oil in a heavy-based saucepan over high heat. Add ginger, garlic and onion and cook, stirring regularly, for 4 minutes or until caramelised.

Add lamb and cook, stirring occasionally, for 2 minutes or until lightly browned.

Add wine or sherry, reduce heat to medium–high and cook for 2 minutes.

Add sugar and 1 tablespoon soy sauce, increase heat to high and cook for 2 minutes or until caramelised. Stir in spice mixture and cook for 1 minute.

Add orange peel and 250 ml (1 cup) water, bring to the boil, then reduce heat to a very gentle simmer. Cover the entire surface with a round of baking paper and simmer gently for 1½ hours or until lamb is tender. There should be only a handful of bubbles breaking the surface. To check if it's ready, pierce the lamb with a small knife – you should meet no resistance.

When the lamb is tender, stir in vinegar, remaining 1 tablespoon soy sauce and the lime juice. Transfer to a bowl and serve.

Serve as part of a banquet for 4

CRISPY ORANGE-PEEL BEEF

Chewy, crispy yet tender pieces of beef with a sticky caramel sauce; the pleasant bitterness of fresh orange peel; the smoky and spicy scents of Sichuan pepper and dried chilli all go toward making this a mysterious and exotic dish. Make sure you have everything ready to go before you coat and fry the brisket, as this is best eaten while still piping-hot and crunchy. The final squeeze of lemon juice on serving just tips it over the edge!

3.5 litres Red Braise Master Stock (page 39)
1 × 450 g piece beef brisket, halved
3 tablespoons cornflour
vegetable oil, for deep-frying
2 egg whites
1 teaspoon peanut oil
8 dried small chillies
5 cm × 3 cm knob (25 g) ginger, finely sliced
3 garlic cloves, finely sliced
2 large strips (about 8 cm × 3 cm) orange peel, white pith removed, cut into fine julienne strips, plus extra to garnish, if desired
1 teaspoon dried chilli flakes
pinch Sichuan Pepper and Salt (page 306)
1 lemon, halved (optional)

Make the red braise master stock in a large saucepan.

Meanwhile, place brisket in a saucepan, cover with cold water and bring to the boil. Simmer for 10 minutes, then rinse well and drain. This will remove any impurities from the meat.

When the stock is ready, return it to the boil. Lower brisket into stock, ensuring it is fully submerged – you may need to weight it down with a plate – and poach brisket gently for 1½–2 hours or until the meat is very tender. There should be no more than an occasional ripple breaking the surface; adjust the temperature, if necessary. Do not put a lid on the pan at any stage. To check if the brisket is ready, pierce it with a small knife – you should meet no resistance.

Remove brisket from stock and refrigerate to cool completely. Reserve 125 ml (½ cup) stock. (Don't forget you can strain and freeze the rest of the master stock to use again.)

Heat reserved stock with 125 ml (½ cup) water in a wok over high heat. Cook for 4 minutes or until reduced by two-thirds. Set aside.

When chilled, pull brisket apart into large bite-sized chunks and dust lightly with cornflour.

Pour enough oil for deep-frying into a wok and heat until the surface seems to shimmer slightly (190°C). Beat egg whites into soft peaks. Working in two batches, dip brisket in egg white, shaking off excess, and deep-fry for 2 minutes or until golden all over, using tongs to turn and separate any pieces that stick together. Remove and drain on kitchen paper. When all the brisket has been deep-fried, carefully discard oil and wipe wok clean.

Heat 1 teaspoon peanut oil in the cleaned wok until the surface seems to shimmer slightly. Add dried chillies and stir-fry for 20 seconds to blacken, then remove from wok. Add ginger and garlic and stir-fry for 1½ minutes to caramelise.

Add brisket, orange peel, chilli flakes and blackened dried chillies to wok and stir-fry for 1 minute. Add reduced stock and toss for 30 seconds to coat brisket.

Transfer to a platter, garnish with Sichuan pepper and salt and serve immediately. Squeeze over lemon juice and top with extra strips of orange peel, if desired.

Serve as part of banquet for 4

STEAMED BEEF BALLS WITH ORANGE PEEL

I've always enjoyed the steamed beef balls served at yum cha – particularly their juiciness and light texture. This is achieved by using fatty beef mince, then stretching the protein in the meat by slapping it against the side of the bowl. The addition of citrus peel makes for an unusual and delicious flavour that permeates the meat – and during the steaming, a wonderfully rich stock comes out of the beef balls, making a perfect light sauce.

500 g minced beef
5 cm × 2 cm knob (20 g) ginger, finely diced
2 garlic cloves, finely diced
1 egg
2 tablespoons light soy sauce
1 tablespoon shao hsing wine or dry sherry
2 teaspoons white sugar
1 bunch coriander, leaves picked, half left whole and half roughly chopped
1 orange
60 g (½ cup) drained Pickled Carrot (page 253), to serve

Serve as a starter for 4–6 (makes 20)

❶ Take small handfuls of the minced beef and slap it against the side of a large bowl. This 'works' the protein, which will tenderise the meat.

❷ Add all remaining ingredients except orange, whole coriander leaves and pickled carrot.

❸ Position a fine grater (a Microplane is ideal) over the bowl and grate the orange zest directly over it, being sure to catch all the citrus oil in the bowl.

❹ Mix thoroughly using your hands. >

❺ Scoop up 1 tablespoon of the mixture.

❻ Roll gently between wet palms to form a ball.

❼ Repeat with remaining mixture to make 20 beef balls in total.

❽ Arrange the beef balls in a shallow heatproof bowl that will fit inside a steamer basket. (You may need to steam them in two batches, depending on the size of your steamer.) Bring a large saucepan or wok of water to the boil. Place bowl inside steamer and cover with the lid. Position over the pan or wok of boiling water and steam for 7–8 minutes or until the balls are cooked – the juices will leach out of the beef balls to form a light sauce.

❾ Remove bowl from steamer, garnish beef balls with coriander leaves and serve with pickled carrot.

STIR-FRIED LAMB WITH BAMBOO SHOOTS AND CHINESE MUSHROOMS

Lamb is used extensively in northern China. And bamboo, with its grassy flavour and robust quality, goes very well with meat, drinking up all the stir-frying juices. If you can't find fresh bamboo, I suggest you use celery instead, slicing it finely on the diagonal. You can also substitute fresh mushrooms for the dried Chinese mushrooms: add 6 fresh shiitake mushrooms (leave them whole, but discard their woody stems) or 100 g roughly torn black cloud ear fungus to the wok along with the soy sauce mixture.

450 g lamb fillet (backstrap), cut into 1 cm thick slices on the diagonal
1 tablespoon light soy sauce
1 teaspoon malt vinegar
1 teaspoon brown sugar
2 tablespoons peanut oil
5 cm × 4 cm knob (30 g) ginger, finely sliced
3 Braised Chinese Mushrooms (page 220), finely sliced
500 g Blanched Bamboo Shoots (page 223)
2 tablespoons shao hsing wine or dry sherry

MARINADE

2 tablespoons light soy sauce
1 tablespoon shao hsing wine or dry sherry
1 tablespoon brown sugar
1 teaspoon sesame oil

Combine lamb with marinade ingredients in a bowl and toss to coat well. Cover and leave to marinate in the refrigerator for at least 2 hours or overnight.

Combine soy sauce, vinegar and sugar in a bowl.

Heat half of the oil in a hot wok until the surface seems to shimmer slightly. Add half of the marinated lamb to wok, reserving marinade in the bowl, and cook for 30 seconds on each side to brown. Remove from wok with a slotted spoon and set aside. Repeat with remaining lamb in the same oil. Remove lamb from wok and set aside.

Wipe wok clean and return to heat. Heat remaining 1 tablespoon oil, add ginger, Chinese mushrooms and bamboo shoots and stir-fry for 2 minutes to warm vegetables through.

Add reserved marinade and wine or sherry to wok and cook for 30 seconds. Add soy sauce mixture and cook for 1 minute or until sauce is caramelised and slightly thickened.

Return lamb to wok and stir-fry for 1 minute to combine. Transfer to a platter and serve immediately.

Serve as part of a banquet for 4

WHITE-COOKED PORK BELLY WITH PICKLES AND BLISTERED CHILLIES

This dish was inspired by the Italian dish of *bollito misto* ('boiled meats'), which is traditionally served with *salsa verde* ('green sauce') and *salsa rosso* ('red sauce'). Pork belly is an extremely popular cut of the pig in the Chinese kitchen, prized for its gelatinous quality and versatility. In this recipe I braise it in a white master stock then serve it warm or at room temperature with seared chillies and pungent, acidic pickles – any of the pickles in this book would work equally well. Alternatively, cook the pork in Red Braise Master Stock (page 39), which would give you a luscious, deep-red colour and a stronger flavour. You could also serve this pork cold and sliced super-thin, like a cold-cuts plate.

1 × 450 g piece free-range pork belly, skin on, at room temperature
3.5 litres White Master Stock (page 36)
80 ml (⅓ cup) Chilli–Soy Dipping Sauce (page 301), optional
1 tablespoon peanut oil
3 large red chillies, smashed with the flat of a knife
30 g (¼ cup) drained Pickled Beetroot (page 246)
30 g (¼ cup) drained Pickled Cucumber (page 250)

Make the white master stock in a large saucepan that will hold the pork belly comfortably.

Meanwhile, place pork belly in a saucepan, cover with cold water and bring to the boil. Simmer for 10 minutes, then rinse well and drain. This will remove any impurities from the meat.

When master stock is ready, return it to the boil. Lower pork into stock, ensuring it is fully submerged – you may need to weight it down with a plate – and poach pork gently for 3 hours or until the meat is very tender. There should be no more than an occasional ripple breaking the surface; adjust the temperature, if necessary. Do not put a lid on the pan at any stage. (Depending on the size of your pan, you may need to top up the stock with hot water during cooking to keep the pork submerged.) To check if it's ready, pierce the pork with a small knife – you should meet no resistance.

Heat peanut oil in a hot wok until the surface seems to shimmer slightly. Add chillies and cook for 30 seconds each side to blister and slightly blacken. Remove with tongs and drain on kitchen paper.

Remove pork from pan and discard stock. Using a large sharp knife, carefully cut pork into 8 mm–1 cm thick slices, trying to keep each slice intact. Arrange on a platter and serve warm, garnished with blistered chillies and with side dishes of pickles.

You can also serve this as a cold meat plate. Simply chill overnight, then cut into slices and bring to room temperature before serving.

Serve as part of a banquet for 4–6

CRYSTAL ROCK SUGAR PORK HOCK

This dish is for when you feel like a lazy afternoon at home, since it requires regular attention, with the basting and turning of the pork hock, but is otherwise undemanding. Your reward is a grand-looking dish that needs nothing more than steamed rice and a plate of Chinese greens. Yellow or golden crystal rock sugar is a type of sugar that comes in the form of large crystals: use a mortar and pestle or a rolling pin to break it down into smaller, more manageable pieces for even cooking. It is readily available in all Chinese grocery stores, and leaves braised meats, stocks and sauces with a stunning, lacquer-like glaze, while imparting a gentle sweetness. In this dish, the sweetness is perfectly balanced by the saltiness of soy sauce and the acidity of vinegar.

1 × 1.7 kg free-range pork hock, skin on and untrimmed
150 g yellow rock sugar
8 cm × 5 cm knob (50 g) ginger, finely sliced
4 spring onions, halved crossways
250 ml (1 cup) shao hsing wine or dry sherry
160 ml (⅔ cup) light soy sauce
160 ml (⅔ cup) malt vinegar

Place pork hock in a large stockpot, cover with plenty of cold water and bring to the boil. Simmer for 10 minutes, then rinse well and drain. This will remove any impurities from the meat.

Meanwhile, loosely wrap rock sugar in a clean tea towel and bash with a rolling pin until roughly crushed.

Add sugar and remaining ingredients, together with 750 ml (3 cups) water, to a large, heavy-based pan that will snugly fit the pork hock and bring to the boil. Add pork hock, reduce heat to a gentle simmer so that there are bubbles just breaking around the hock. Cover with a lid and braise for 2–2½ hours or until the meat is very tender, turning it every 20–30 minutes and basting with the braising liquid. Top up with boiling water as necessary to keep the lower third of the pork covered throughout the cooking time. To check if the pork is ready, pierce the meat with a small knife – you should meet no resistance.

Transfer the pork hock to a serving platter, strain the braising liquid and pour over the meat.

Serve as part of a banquet for 6–8

STEAMED PORK SPARE-RIBS WITH BLACK BEAN AND GINGER

I can never resist this if it's on the yum cha trolley. This dish only works when you marinate the pork overnight – this gives the black bean, ginger and chilli time to really work their magic on the pork, and for the shao hsing wine to tenderise the meat and add an incredible depth of flavour. Use a chef's knife or cleaver to chop up the spare ribs, or get your butcher to do this for you. It's important to use pork belly on the bone, because this adds to the overall taste and juiciness of the dish.

700 g free-range pork spare-ribs (pork belly with bones), cut into 3 cm pieces
5 cm × 5 cm knob (35 g) ginger, cut into fine julienne strips
4 garlic cloves, finely diced
1 large red chilli, finely sliced
80 ml (⅓ cup) shao hsing wine or dry sherry
2 tablespoons salted black beans
2 tablespoons light soy sauce
3 teaspoons white sugar
2 teaspoons peanut oil
2 teaspoon sesame oil
2 teaspoons malt vinegar

TO GARNISH
1 large red chilli, finely sliced

Combine all of the ingredients except the garnish in a large bowl and, using your hands, massage the marinade thoroughly into the ribs. Cover and refrigerate overnight to marinate and tenderise the meat.

Bring a large saucepan or wok of water to the boil.

Place pork and marinade in a shallow heatproof bowl that will fit inside a steamer basket. Place bowl inside steamer and cover with the lid. Position over the pan or wok of boiling water and steam for 25 minutes or until pork is tender, using tongs to turn the pork pieces halfway through the cooking time.

Transfer pork and cooking juices to a serving bowl, garnish with chilli and serve immediately.

Serve as a main course for 2 or as part of a banquet for 4

RED-BRAISED PORK BELLY WITH EGGS, CARROT AND SHALLOTS

This is a little like a Chinese casserole: a wonderful wintry dish that, with the addition of a bowl of steamed rice, provides a substantial and comforting meal. It is as amenable as a casserole too, so you can cook it the day before then reheat it when you want to serve it. The slow-braised carrots and shallots become deliciously sweet and tender. For a less hearty version, just leave out the boiled eggs. Feel free to include other vegetables, such as white radish (daikon), cauliflower florets or mushrooms – and don't forget that you can strain and freeze the red braise master stock to use again.

- **3.5 litres Red Braise Master Stock (page 39)**
- **450 g free-range boneless pork belly, skin on, at room temperature, cut into 2 cm pieces**
- **4 free-range eggs, at room temperature**
- **3–4 carrots, halved if large**
- **4 red shallots, peeled but left whole**
- **1 tablespoon dark brown sugar**
- **1 teaspoon light soy sauce**
- **1 teaspoon malt vinegar**
- **¼ teaspoon sesame oil**

Make the red braise master stock in a stockpot that will fit the pork, eggs, carrots and shallots.

Meanwhile, place pork belly in a large saucepan, cover with cold water and bring to the boil. Simmer for 10 minutes, then drain. This will remove any impurities from the meat.

Place eggs in a small saucepan of boiling water and cook for 7 minutes (or 8 minutes, if using eggs straight from the fridge). Remove eggs using a slotted spoon and refresh under cold water. Carefully peel eggs and drain on kitchen paper to remove excess liquid.

When the stock is ready, return it to the boil. Add pork, eggs, carrots and shallots, cover the entire surface with a round of baking paper and simmer gently for 45 minutes or until pork is tender. There should be no more than an occasional ripple breaking the surface; adjust the temperature, if necessary. To check if it's ready, pierce the pork with a small knife – you should meet no resistance.

When the pork is just about ready, scoop out 250 ml (1 cup) stock from the pork and place in a small saucepan. Add sugar, soy sauce, vinegar and sesame oil and cook over medium–high heat for 5 minutes or until sauce is reduced by half and syrupy.

Using a slotted spoon, lift out the pork belly, carrots, shallots and braising aromatics from the stockpot and place on a large platter. Scoop out the eggs and cut in half. Spoon the sauce over the pork and arrange the egg halves on top to serve.

(Don't forget you can strain and freeze the master stock to use again.)

Serves as part of a banquet for 6

RED-BRAISED PORK BELLY WITH GREEN CHILLIES AND GARLIC

This combination of pork and green chillies is very common in China, particularly in the south-west. Stir-frying the green chillies with a hint of vinegar and sugar transforms them into tasty little morsels that go beautifully with the rich pork.

3.5 litres Red Braise Master Stock (page 39)
1 × 450 g free-range boneless pork belly, skin on, at room temperature
2 teaspoons light soy sauce
1 teaspoon malt vinegar
½ teaspoon brown sugar
1 tablespoon peanut oil
5 cm × 2 cm knob (20 g) ginger, finely sliced
2 garlic cloves, crushed
3 large green chillies, thickly sliced on the diagonal

Make the red braise master stock in a large saucepan that will hold the pork belly comfortably.

Meanwhile, place pork belly in a saucepan, cover with plenty of cold water and bring to the boil. Simmer for 10 minutes, then drain. This will remove any impurities from the meat.

When the stock is ready, return it to the boil. Lower pork belly into the stock, ensuring it is fully submerged – you may need to weight it down with a plate – and poach pork gently for 3 hours or until the meat is very tender. There should be no more than an occasional ripple breaking the surface; adjust the temperature, if necessary. Do not put a lid on the pan at any stage. (Depending on the size of your pan, you may need to top up the stock with hot water during cooking to keep the pork submerged.) To check if it's ready, pierce the pork with a small knife – you should meet no resistance.

Remove pork from pan and reserve 125 ml (½ cup) stock. (Don't forget you can strain and freeze the rest of the master stock to use again.) When pork is cool enough to handle, carefully cut into large bite-sized pieces.

Heat reserved stock with 125 ml (½ cup) water in a wok over high heat and cook for 4 minutes or until reduced by two-thirds. Add pork to reduced sauce in wok, turn heat down to medium–high and stir-fry for 2 minutes to warm through.

Meanwhile, combine soy sauce, vinegar and sugar in a bowl. Heat oil in a frying pan until surface seems to shimmer slightly. Add ginger, garlic and chilli and cook, stirring regularly, for 1½ minutes to blister the chilli and caramelise the garlic. Add soy sauce mixture and cook, stirring regularly, for 1 minute or until sauce is slightly thickened.

Serve pork in a large bowl, topped with the chilli and soy sauce mixture.

Serve as part of a banquet for 4

ROASTED PORK SHOULDER WITH MISO AND HONEY

This is my version of traditional Chinese BBQ pork. I use miso a lot in my cooking, finding its salty flavour and thick consistency a good substitute for some other Asian condiments, such as hoisin sauce, that all too often are laden with preservatives and other chemicals. Here the saltiness of the miso is balanced by the sweetness of honey, which also helps to create the sticky coating that we all find so irresistible about the BBQ pork from Chinatown. Any leftovers can be used in Home-Style Fried Eggs with Roasted Pork (page 177), Fried Rice with Roasted Pork (page 269) or Thin Egg Noodle Salad with Roasted Pork, Pickled Carrot and Sesame Seeds (page 274) the next day.

---

2 × 500 g pieces free-range boneless pork shoulder

MARINADE

6 cm × 5 cm knob (40 g) ginger, finely diced
6 garlic cloves, finely diced
3 tablespoons shao hsing wine or dry sherry
2½ tablespoons honey
1½ tablespoons brown rice miso paste
2 teaspoons light soy sauce
1 teaspoon five-spice powder
½ teaspoon sesame oil
½ teaspoon Sichuan pepper

Combine pork and marinade ingredients in a large bowl and refrigerate overnight to marinate.

The next day, bring pork to room temperature and preheat oven to 190°C.

Remove pork from marinade, reserving marinade. Place pork, fat-side up, on a wire rack in a roasting tray and pour in 250 ml (1 cup) water.

Roast pork for 45 minutes, basting every 15 minutes with a generous amount of the reserved marinade.

After 45 minutes, increase oven temperature to 220°C and continue to roast pork for a further 10 minutes.

Remove pork from oven and allow to rest, uncovered, in a warm place for 15 minutes.

To serve, cut into 1 cm thick slices.

Serve as part of a banquet for 6–8

PORK PATTIES WITH SESAME AND GARLIC VINAIGRETTE

These patties are a delicious mouthful, and make a perfect appetiser at a dinner or lunch party. Only ever use fatty pork mince (ideally from belly pork) for these, to ensure tenderness and juiciness; otherwise, they will be dry and unpalatable. The sesame and garlic vinaigrette is acidic and nutty in flavour and works very well with the rich pork.

vegetable oil, for deep-frying
60 g (½ cup) cornflour
1 tablespoon roasted sesame seeds

SESAME AND GARLIC VINAIGRETTE
2 garlic cloves, finely diced
1 teaspoon white sugar
1 tablespoon light soy sauce
3 tablespoons sesame oil
2 tablespoons malt vinegar

PORK PATTIES
450 g minced pork belly
5 cm × 2 cm knob (20 g) ginger, finely diced
2 garlic cloves, finely diced
2 spring onions, finely sliced
1 large red shallot, finely chopped
½ bunch coriander, stems only, finely chopped
½ bunch mint, leaves picked and roughly chopped
¼ bunch dill, stems only, finely chopped
2 tablespoons light soy sauce
1 tablespoons shao hsing wine or dry sherry
1 teaspoon white sugar
1 teaspoon sesame oil
1 egg

First make the sesame and garlic vinaigrette. Place garlic and sugar in a bowl and whisk well to combine. Whisk in soy sauce, then while whisking, slowly drizzle in sesame oil and whisk until combined. Whisk in vinegar to finish. Set aside until required, giving it another whisk just before using.

To make the pork patties, take small handfuls of minced pork and slap against the side of a large bowl in order to work the protein, which will tenderise the meat. Add remaining ingredients and mix thoroughly using your hands.

Scoop up 1 tablespoon of pork mixture and roll gently between wet palms to form a ball, then flatten slightly into an 8 mm thick patty – this will help the patties to cook evenly (they will spring back as they cook). Place on a tray or plate lined with baking paper and repeat with remaining mixture.

Heat a 3 cm depth of oil in a hot wok until surface seems to shimmer slightly (190°C). Lightly dust half of the pork patties in cornflour, shaking off any excess, then carefully slide into the hot oil. Deep-fry for 3 minutes or until golden all over and cooked through. Remove using a slotted spoon and drain on kitchen paper. Repeat with remaining patties.

Arrange pork patties on a serving platter, sprinkle with sesame seeds and serve with a side dish of sesame and garlic vinaigrette.

Serve as a starter for 4–6 (makes 20)

BARBECUED PORK RIBS

Be sure to ask your butcher for 'USA-style' pork ribs for this recipe: these are the big, long-boned ones that are great for barbecuing, eating with your fingers, and wrapping your jaws around. This marinade is big and robust, with plenty of homemade chilli and dark brown sugar for extra caramelisation. Ask the butcher to separate the ribs too, so the marinade can really get into each one and, for the very best flavour, do try and leave these to marinate overnight. The cucumber and lemon provide cool relief and add zing to these sticky, spicy ribs.

700 g free-range pork ribs (USA-style), ribs separated
2 tablespoons vegetable oil, for brushing
1 small cucumber, cut into wedges
1 lemon, halved

MARINADE

3 tablespoons light soy sauce
3 tablespoons red wine
2 tablespoons Chilli Sauce (page 297)
2 tablespoons dark brown sugar
1 tablespoon peanut oil
2 teaspoons malt vinegar
1 teaspoon sesame oil
5 cm × 3 cm knob (25 g) ginger, finely diced
3 garlic cloves, finely diced
½ teaspoons Sichuan Pepper and Salt (page 306)

STICKY SAUCE

1 tablespoon light soy sauce
1 tablespoon dark brown sugar
1 teaspoon malt vinegar

Combine all of the marinade ingredients in a large bowl. Add the ribs and, using your hands, massage the marinade thoroughly into the ribs. Cover and refrigerate overnight.

Heat a barbecue or chargrill pan to moderate heat and lightly brush with vegetable oil. Place ribs on grill or in pan, reserving marinade, and cook for 5 minutes.

After 5 minutes, baste ribs with a little of the reserved marinade, turn over, cover with the hood or a lid and cook on the other side for 3 minutes.

Meanwhile, make the sticky sauce. Place remaining marinade in a saucepan over medium–high heat. Add soy sauce, sugar and vinegar and bring to the boil, stirring to dissolve sugar. Cook for 3 minutes or until reduced by half and sticky.

Arrange ribs on a serving platter and spoon over the sauce. Serve with fresh cucumber and lemon halves for squeezing over.

Serve as a starter for 2 or as a snack for 4

CRISPY SOY-ROASTED PORK BELLY

Everyone I know just loves pork crackling, and this recipe results in a great layer of crackling. To get good crackling, it's important to follow the steps here closely, especially the initial scalding of the skin, and then allowing the pork to thoroughly dry out, uncovered in the refrigerator, after it has marinated.

---

1 × 800 g piece free-range boneless pork belly, skin on and scored (ask your butcher to do this)
500 ml (2 cups) boiling water
1 tablespoon sesame oil
1 tablespoon salt flakes

MARINADE
2 tablespoons brown rice miso paste
1 tablespoon five-spice powder
1 tablespoon brown sugar
1 tablespoon light soy sauce

Place pork belly, skin-side up, on a wire rack over the sink. Pour over boiling water to scald the pork skin – this will help the skin crisp up into crunchy crackling. Pat rind thoroughly dry with kitchen paper and place pork, uncovered, in refrigerator for 2 hours.

Remove pork from fridge and place, skin-side up, on a chopping board. Using the tip of a sharp knife, stab the pork skin repeatedly until the surface is covered with holes, being careful not to go all the way through. Turn the pork belly over and make cuts about 2 cm apart and 1 cm deep.

Combine marinade ingredients in a bowl and mix well. Rub marinade evenly over the flesh side of the pork (not the skin) and massage well into the cuts.

Place pork, skin-side up, on a wire rack (this same rack will be used for roasting the pork, so make sure it is ovenproof and fits inside a roasting tin) and place over a tray or large plate to catch any drips. Place in refrigerator and leave pork uncovered overnight, during which time the skin will dry out. The drier the skin, the better the crackling when roasted.

The next day, bring pork to room temperature and preheat oven to 150°C.

Transfer pork and wire rack to a roasting tin. Rub skin well with the sesame oil, then scatter salt all over. Roast for 1½–2 hours or until tender (to test, pierce the meat with a skewer – you should meet no resistance). Increase the oven temperature to 220°C and continue roasting for 15 minutes. This final blast of heat will crisp up the skin, turning it into crackling.

Remove pork from oven and allow to rest, uncovered, in a warm place for 15 minutes.

To serve, cut into 1 cm thick slices.

Serve as part of a banquet for 4

STIR-FRIED PORK AND CLAMS WITH BLACK BEANS

I just love clams, and whenever I am in Italy I always indulge in many plates of clams with prosciutto, white wine and garlic. With its combination of pork and seafood, this dish shares elements of this Italian classic – as do many Chinese dishes, I have realised. The pungent, distinctive aroma and flavour of salted black beans is a perfect counterpoint to the salty, oceanic taste of the clams.

1 kg baby clams
1 tablespoon light soy sauce
1 tablespoon malt vinegar
1 teaspoon brown sugar
1 teaspoon sesame oil
2 tablespoons peanut oil
5 cm × 2 cm knob (20 g) ginger, roughly diced
3 garlic cloves, roughly diced
2 tablespoons salted black beans
200 g minced pork belly
3 tablespoons shao hsing wine or dry sherry
2 red shallots, halved and finely sliced
2 spring onions, finely sliced

Soak clams in plenty of cold water for 2 hours, changing the water every 30 minutes. This will help purge the clams of any grit. Drain.

Bring 125 ml (½ cup) water to the boil in a wok over high heat. Add clams and cover. After 1–2 minutes, the clams should start opening. As they begin to open, immediately remove them from wok with tongs and place in a bowl. You can use your tongs to tap on the shells to encourage them to open up, but discard any that have not opened after about 5 minutes. Drain water from wok and wipe clean with kitchen paper.

Combine soy sauce, vinegar, sugar and sesame oil in a small bowl.

Heat peanut oil in the hot wok until the surface seems to shimmer slightly. Add ginger, garlic and black beans and stir-fry for 30 seconds, stirring constantly to ensure the black beans don't burn.

Add pork and stir-fry for 2 minutes or until just browned. Add wine or sherry and cook for 30 seconds.

Return clams to the wok, add soy sauce mixture and shallot and stir-fry for 2 minutes or until sauce is slightly thickened.

Remove from the heat and toss through the spring onion. Transfer to a large platter and serve immediately.

Serve as part of a banquet for 4

SEAFOOD

SASHIMI OF SNAPPER WITH CHILLI–LIME DRESSING

I could happily eat sashimi every day of my life. With such pristine, clean and well-managed fisheries in Australia, we are so fortunate to enjoy the highest-quality seafood. Seek out the freshest piece of snapper you can find for this simple yet stunning recipe – or choose another suitable fish, such as bream, King George whiting, ocean trout or salmon. This chilli–lime dressing works well with any type of seafood: try it with grilled prawns or roast ocean trout.

1 × 300 g piece sashimi-grade snapper fillet
pinch Sichuan Pepper and Salt (page 306), optional

CHILLI–LIME DRESSING
1½ teaspoons light soy sauce
1 teaspoon grapeseed oil
½ teaspoon white sugar
½ teaspoon dried chilli flakes
¼ teaspoon sesame oil
juice of ½ lime

Using a very sharp knife, cut fish into 5 mm thick slices on the diagonal and arrange on a platter.

Place the dressing ingredients in a bowl and whisk until well combined.

Drizzle dressing over snapper and garnish with Sichuan pepper and salt, if using.

Serve as a starter for 2–4

TEA-SMOKED OYSTERS

I first learnt this technique when I was working for Neil Perry. Based on a traditional Chinese method of tea-smoking, it adds an exotic and complex flavour to all kinds of seafood, poultry and meat. Be warned, though: the smoke billowing from the wok can be incredibly strong and overpowering, so make sure you do this under an efficient range-hood extractor in a well-ventilated kitchen, and keep a safe distance away from any smoke alarms. These tea-smoked oysters are delicious eaten alone as a snack, added to a salad, or with meat dishes. Stored in an airtight container with their cooking juices under a layer of vegetable oil, they will keep in the refrigerator for up to a week.

---

12 freshly shucked oysters
125 ml (½ cup) vegetable oil, or enough to cover

SMOKING MIXTURE
3 tablespoons jasmine tea leaves
3 tablespoons brown sugar
3 tablespoons jasmine rice

Makes 12

Use in • Stir-Fried Chicken with Tea-Smoked Oysters and Pickled Chillies (page 69)

1 First, make a 'boat' for the smoking mixture to sit in. Fold a 30 cm x 45 cm piece of foil in half crossways, then fold up each edge to make a 5 cm rim.

2 Place the tea leaves, sugar and rice in a bowl to make the smoking mixture.

3 Combine well using your hands.

4 Spread the smoking mixture evenly over the base of the boat, then place in a hot wok. >

5 Heat for about 2 minutes or until the mixture begins to smoke a lot.

6 Sit oysters in a steamer basket and cover with lid. When the smoking mixture is billowing, carefully place steamer basket in wok and smoke oysters for 6–7½ minutes.

7 Check to see if oysters are ready – they should be lightly caramel in colour. Be careful of the hot smoke when checking for doneness.

8 Carefully remove steamer basket from wok. Remove boat of smoking mixture and submerge completely in a tub of cold water to extinguish before discarding.

FRIED OYSTERS WITH CHILLI SALT AND PICKLED RED ONION

Gorgeous little mouthfuls of heaven – that's exactly what these fried oysters are to me! Cook them just before serving, because they are definitely best eaten straightaway, while they're still hot and crunchy. Biting through the surprisingly delicate beer batter into a silky, smooth, juicy oyster is very special. I serve these with pickled onion and lemon, the sourness adding a much-needed kick to the creamy, naturally rich oysters.

12 freshly shucked oysters
3 tablespoons cornflour
vegetable oil, for deep-frying
1 tablespoon Chilli Salt (page 305)
65 g (½ cup) drained Pickled Red Onion (page 245)
lemon wedges, to serve

BEER BATTER
2 tablespoons beer
2 tablespoons plain flour
2 ice cubes

Remove the oysters from their shells and place on kitchen paper to drain.

To make the beer batter, combine the ingredients in a bowl with a slotted spoon (using this rather than a whisk keeps the batter thick and lumpy, and the lumps become crunchy when deep-fried). Leave batter at room temperature for 3–5 minutes or until the ice has half melted – it should be the consistency of runny custard. (You may need to add a little more flour to the batter if it's too runny – it all depends on the humidity.) Use batter immediately.

Pour enough oil for deep-frying into a wok and heat until the surface seems to shimmer slightly (190°C). Working quickly, cover a large plate with cornflour, place oysters in flour and shake plate to lightly coat each oyster, using your fingers to turn the oysters and shake off any excess. Place oysters in batter and, using wooden chopsticks, turn to coat completely, shaking off any excess. Carefully – they will spit – drop each oyster into the hot oil and deep-fry for about 40 seconds or until lightly browned, turning halfway through. You may need to do this in two batches.

Remove the fried oysters with a slotted spoon and drain well on kitchen paper. Arrange on a platter and serve immediately with chilli salt, pickled red onion and lemon wedges for squeezing over.

Serve as a starter for 2

CRISPY PRAWN CAKES WITH CHILLI–VINEGAR DIPPING SAUCE

The Chinese are very inventive when it comes to tasty little morsels, such as these crispy prawn cakes. I add fine julienne strips of carrot for colour and texture, and a pleasingly rustic appearance. Although the egg acts as a binding agent, the prawn cakes are still very delicate, so do be extra-careful when handling them, especially when turning them over in the frying pan.

800 g uncooked prawns, peeled and deveined (about 380 g prawn meat)
3 cm × 2 cm knob (10 g) ginger, finely diced
½ bunch coriander, stems and roots only, washed and finely sliced
2 spring onions, finely sliced
1 small stick celery, finely diced
½ small carrot, cut into fine julienne strips
1¼ tablespoons light soy sauce
1 tablespoon shao hsing wine or dry sherry
¼ teaspoon sesame oil
1 teaspoon white sugar
1 egg
2 tablespoons vegetable oil
125 ml (½ cup) Chilli–Vinegar Dipping Sauce (page 302)

Roughly chop the prawn meat and place in a large bowl. Add all the remaining ingredients except the vegetable oil and dipping sauce, and mix thoroughly using your hands.

Heat half of the vegetable oil in a large non-stick frying pan over medium–high heat. Add heaped tablespoonfuls of prawn mixture to the pan, taking care not to crowd the pan. Cook for about 1–1½ minutes or until golden, then carefully turn over and cook the other side for about 1–1½ minutes or until golden and cooked through. Carefully remove from the pan and drain on kitchen paper. Wipe pan clean and repeat with remaining vegetable oil and prawn mixture.

Arrange prawn cakes on a large platter in a single layer so they don't become soggy in their own steam. Serve immediately with a side dish of dipping sauce for spooning over.

Serve as a starter for 4 (makes 16)

STEAMED SCALLOPS WITH GINGER AND SPRING ONION

The classic Cantonese flavour combination of ginger and spring onion is one I grew up with, and still use extensively in my cooking. It goes perfectly with seafood, particularly oysters, scallops and fish. For this recipe, I steam the scallops in their shell to catch all the delicious scallop and cooking juices. Scallops need very little cooking time – I like mine still slightly glassy in the centre. The hot peanut oil is a very important element, scalding the raw ginger and spring onion, as is dissolving the sugar in the soy sauce and shao hsing wine to create a sublime sauce.

6 scallops on the half shell
1 tablespoon shao hsing wine or dry sherry
3 cm × 2 cm knob (20 g) ginger, cut into fine julienne strips
½ teaspoon white sugar
1 tablespoon light soy sauce
¼ teaspoon sesame oil
1 tablespoon peanut oil
2 spring onions, cut into fine julienne strips
pinch freshly ground white pepper
½ bunch coriander, leaves picked

Bring a large saucepan or wok of water to the boil.

Arrange scallops, shell-side down, in a single layer in a heatproof shallow bowl that will fit inside a large steamer basket. You may need to overlap the shells, but make sure the scallops are not covered. Pour wine or sherry over scallops, then sprinkle with the ginger.

Place bowl inside steamer and cover with the lid. Position over the pan or wok of boiling water and steam for 3–4 minutes or until scallops are just cooked.

Using tongs, carefully remove scallops, being careful not to spill any of the cooking juices in the shell, and arrange on a serving platter. Pour any liquid left in the bowl over the scallops, sprinkle over sugar, drizzle with combined soy sauce and sesame oil, then scatter over spring onion.

Heat peanut oil in a small saucepan until moderately hot, then carefully pour over scallops. Sprinkle with pepper, scatter over coriander and serve immediately.

Serve as a starter for 2

STIR-FRIED SCALLOPS WITH XO SAUCE

Another Chinese classic combination: seafood with XO sauce. The scallops are naturally rich and juicy enough to handle this very confident and robust chilli sauce. Make sure you have plenty of steamed rice handy to soak up all the rich, luscious XO sauce. You could use fresh prawns instead of scallops here.

3 tablespoons XO Sauce (page 298)
1 tablespoon light soy sauce
1 teaspoon white sugar
2 large red chillies
1 tablespoon peanut oil
24 scallops, removed from their shells (about 240 g scallop meat)
5 cm × 2 cm knob (20 g) ginger, cut into fine julienne strips
3 tablespoons shao hsing wine or dry sherry
1 tablespoon stock or water
1 teaspoon malt vinegar
½ teaspoon sesame oil
pinch Sichuan Pepper and Salt (page 306)

Combine XO sauce, soy sauce and sugar in a small bowl and set aside.

Trim stems off chillies, cut in half lengthways and remove seeds with a spoon.

Heat peanut oil in a hot wok until the surface seems to shimmer slightly. Add chilli halves and cook for 30 seconds each side to blister and slightly blacken. Remove with tongs and drain on kitchen paper. Reserve oil in wok.

Add scallops to wok, in two batches if necessary, and sear for 30 seconds on one side, then turn over and sear the other side for 10 seconds so they are nicely caramelised. Remove and drain on kitchen paper.

Add ginger to wok and stir-fry for 5 seconds, then add wine or sherry and cook for 30 seconds.

Add XO sauce mixture and cook, stirring occasionally, for 30 seconds to caramelise, then add stock or water and cook for 30 seconds.

Return scallops to wok, along with vinegar and sesame oil, and toss to coat. Transfer to a serving plate, garnish with blistered chillies and sprinkle with Sichuan pepper and salt. Serve immediately.

Serve as part of a banquet for 4–6

STIR-FRIED SCALLOPS WITH SNOW PEAS AND GARLIC

This is a very straightforward stir-fry, the success of which relies entirely on the quality of the ingredients used, so make sure you seek out the best-quality scallops and the freshest snow peas. If you can't find good fresh scallops, use prawns instead. Rather than thickening the sauce with cornflour, I like to simply reduce the sauce by simmering it in the wok, which naturally thickens it.

2 tablespoons light soy sauce
1 teaspoon malt vinegar
1 teaspoon brown sugar
½ teaspoon sesame oil
1 tablespoon peanut oil
24 scallops, removed from their shells (about 240 g scallop meat)
120 g snow peas, topped and tailed
3 spring onions, cut into 7 cm lengths
2 garlic cloves, crushed
2 tablespoons shao hsing wine or dry sherry

Combine soy sauce, vinegar, sugar and sesame oil in a small bowl and set aside.

Heat peanut oil in a hot wok until the surface seems to shimmer slightly. Add scallops to wok, in two batches if necessary, and sear for 30 seconds on one side, then turn over and sear the other side for 10 seconds so they are nicely caramelised. Remove and drain on kitchen paper.

Add snow peas, spring onion and garlic to wok and stir-fry for 30 seconds. Add wine or sherry and cook for 10 seconds.

Return scallops to wok, add soy sauce mixture and stir-fry for 30 seconds. Serve immediately.

Serve as part of a banquet for 4–6

DEEP-FRIED SCHOOL PRAWNS WITH CHILLI SALT AND LEMON

School prawns feature in my childhood memories of family holidays spent in Byron Bay. They are so quintessentially Australian and whenever they are in season, I pounce on them. Be sure to drain and pat the prawns dry with paper towel, otherwise they will spit like mad in the hot oil. These tiny prawns are best eaten while they are hot and crisp. They are so small that you can eat the entire prawn, head and all – a wonderful snack that goes perfectly with an icy-cold beer.

200 g uncooked small school prawns
250 ml (1 cup) vegetable oil, for deep-frying
good pinch Chilli Salt (page 305)
1 lemon, halved

Drain prawns on kitchen paper, patting them thoroughly dry so they won't splatter during cooking.

Pour enough oil for deep-frying into a wok and heat until the surface seems to shimmer slightly (190°C). Carefully add half the prawns and deep-fry, turning occasionally, for 1½ minutes or until golden and crunchy. Remove with a slotted spoon and drain well on kitchen paper. Allow the oil to return to 190°C and repeat with remaining prawns.

Arrange prawns on a platter, sprinkle with chilli salt and squeeze over lemon juice. Serve immediately.

Serve as a starter for 4

STEAMED WHOLE SNAPPER WITH BLACK BEANS AND CHILLI

There are many different ways in the Chinese kitchen to dress steamed fish. This dressing is made from salted black beans, chilli, ginger and garlic, and its pungent flavour seeps right into the flesh of the fish during the cooking process. The resulting juices are amazingly delicious soaked up with steamed rice.

- **1 × 550 g whole snapper, scaled, gutted and cleaned**
- **5 cm × 3 cm knob (25 g) ginger, finely diced**
- **3 garlic cloves, finely diced**
- **2 tablespoons salted black beans**
- **1 teaspoon dried chilli flakes**
- **1 teaspoon white sugar**
- **2 spring onions, cut into 10 cm lengths**
- **3 tablespoons shao hsing wine or dry sherry**
- **2 tablespoons light soy sauce**
- **2 spring onions, extra, finely sliced**
- **2 tablespoons peanut oil**

Bring a large saucepan or wok of water to the boil.

Pat fish dry with kitchen paper and place on a chopping board. Using a sharp knife, make 4 diagonal slits on one side of the fish. Turn fish over and repeat on the other side.

Place fish in a shallow heatproof bowl that will fit inside a steamer basket. Combine ginger, garlic, black beans, chilli flakes and sugar in a bowl and spread mixture evenly over the fish, pressing it into the slits. Tuck the spring onion lengths into the belly and pour wine or sherry over the entire fish.

Place bowl inside steamer and cover with the lid. Position over the pan or wok of boiling water and steam for 8 minutes or until fish is cooked. The flesh should be white; if it is still translucent, cook for another minute or so.

Carefully transfer cooked fish to a serving platter. Pour all the cooking juices over the fish, along with the soy sauce, and scatter with sliced spring onion.

Heat oil in a small saucepan until smoking hot, then pour over the fish to scald and sear the spring onion. Serve immediately.

Serve as part of a banquet for 4

STEAMED MUSSELS WITH SICHUAN CHILLI OIL AND PICKLED CELERY

We are able to buy such beautiful, clean-flavoured mussels in Australia. And if you can find the ones that come packed live in 1 kg bags – already washed, scrubbed and even de-bearded – preparing them couldn't be easier. Mussels cook very quickly, so you need to stand over them with tongs at the ready, picking them out of the boiling water as soon as their shells pop open; there is nothing worse than shrivelled, overcooked mussels. Here the rich, oceanic flavour of mussels is pepped up by a lively Sichuan chilli oil and the crunch of pickled celery offers a welcome contrast to the silky, velvety mussels.

---

1 kg mussels, scrubbed and debearded
pinch Sichuan Pepper and Salt (page 306)

SICHUAN CHILLI OIL
1 teaspoon dried chilli flakes
3 tablespoons vegetable oil
1 tablespoon light soy sauce
1 tablespoon hot water
2 teaspoons malt vinegar
1 teaspoon white sugar

QUICK PICKLED CELERY
3 celery stalks from the heart or 2 regular celery stalks, trimmed and cut into 5 cm long matchsticks
1 teaspoon salt flakes
1 teaspoon white sugar
1 tablespoon malt vinegar

To make the Sichuan chilli oil, place chilli flakes in a heatproof bowl. Heat oil in a small heavy-based saucepan until the surface seems to shimmer slightly. Carefully pour hot oil over chilli to release the heat and flavour. Stir to combine then set aside for at least 30 minutes to cool.

Meanwhile, make the quick pickled celery. Place celery, salt and sugar in a bowl and combine well with your hands. Refrigerate for 30 minutes. Drain celery well, squeezing with your hands to remove any excess liquid, then toss with vinegar.

Strain the cooled Sichuan chilli oil through a sieve placed over a large bowl. Discard half of the chilli flakes and stir the remaining half back into the oil. Whisk in soy sauce, hot water, vinegar and sugar.

Bring 250 ml (1 cup) water to the boil in a wok over high heat. Add mussels and cover. After 1–2 minutes, the mussels should start opening. As they begin to open, immediately remove from wok with tongs and place in a bowl. You can use your tongs to tap on the shells to encourage them to open up but discard any that have not opened after about 5 minutes. Quickly rinse mussels under cold running water until cool enough to handle, then remove the mussel meat.

Add mussels and pickled celery to Sichuan chilli oil and toss to combine. Spoon into a shallow serving bowl, garnish with Sichuan pepper and salt and serve.

Serve as a starter for 2–4

STIR-FRIED BABY CLAMS WITH LUP CHEONG SAUSAGE AND POTATO

This dish reminds me of similar combinations of ingredients found in classic Italian and Spanish cuisines, with their clams, cured meats or sausages and potatoes. The sweetness of the lup cheong sausage works perfectly with the natural saltiness of the clams, and the potato absorbs the delicious cooking juices. Mop up the rest of the juices with steamed rice.

---

1 kg live baby clams
2 tablespoons light soy sauce
1 tablespoon malt vinegar
1 teaspoon brown sugar
1 teaspoon sesame oil
2 tablespoons peanut oil
5 cm × 2 cm (20 g) knob ginger, cut into fine julienne strips
2 garlic cloves, roughly diced
2 lup cheong sausages, cut into matchsticks
1 small potato, peeled and cut into fine julienne strips
3 tablespoons shao hsing wine or dry sherry
1 large red chilli, finely sliced on the diagonal

Soak clams in plenty of cold water for 2 hours, changing the water every 30 minutes. This will help purge the clams of any grit. Drain.

Bring 125 ml (½ cup) water to the boil in a wok over high heat. Add clams and cover. After 1–2 minutes, the clams should start opening. As they begin to open, immediately remove them from wok with tongs and place in a bowl. You can tap on the shells to encourage them to open up, but discard any that have not opened after about 5 minutes. Drain water from wok and wipe clean with kitchen paper.

Combine soy sauce, vinegar, sugar and sesame oil in a small bowl and set aside.

Heat peanut oil in the hot wok until the surface seems to shimmer slightly. Add ginger, garlic, lup cheong and potato and stir-fry for 1½ minutes, making sure the garlic doesn't burn.

Return clams to wok and stir-fry for 30 seconds. Add wine or sherry and cook for 30 seconds. Add soy sauce mixture and chilli and stir-fry for 2 minutes or until sauce is slightly thickened. The potato should be just cooked but still have some bite to it.

Serve immediately on a large platter.

Serve as part of a banquet for 4

FISH FILLETS WITH CHINESE MUSHROOMS AND LUP CHEONG SAUSAGE

This is a great meal-in-a-bowl – just mix everything together and pop it into the steamer. I particularly like the contrasting textures: delicate fish, intensely savoury yet tender Chinese mushrooms, and sweet, chewy lup cheong sausage. My mum often makes this with chicken fillets instead of fish, which is also beautiful.

- **400 g white-fleshed fish fillets, cut into 7 cm chunks**
- **4 small Braised Chinese Mushrooms (page 220), halved on the diagonal**
- **1 lup cheong sausage, finely sliced on the diagonal**
- **5 cm × 2 cm knob (20 g) ginger, cut into fine julienne strips**
- **2 tablespoons shao hsing wine or dry sherry**
- **1 tablespoon light soy sauce**
- **½ teaspoon white sugar**
- **½ teaspoon sesame oil**

Bring a large saucepan or wok of water to the boil.

Place all the ingredients in a shallow heatproof bowl that will fit inside a steamer basket. Gently mix everything together, then place bowl inside steamer and cover with the lid.

Position steamer over the pan or wok of boiling water and steam for 8–9 minutes or until fish is cooked, turning the fish pieces halfway through the cooking time. The fish is ready when the flesh is white; if it is still translucent, cook for another minute or so. Serve immediately.

Serve as part of a banquet for 4

SUNG CHOI BAO OF SEAFOOD

There is nothing more satisfying than piping-hot, tasty morsels wrapped in a cold, crisp iceberg lettuce cup and eaten with your fingers. Although this classic Cantonese dish is traditionally made with pork, I like to do variations on the theme, whether it be a vegetarian version or this one, made with a variety of fresh seafood. You could also use chunks of lobster meat, blue eye, snapper or bream, or even make a chicken version with finely diced chicken thigh fillets. The addition of finely sliced raw carrot, Chinese cabbage and bean sprouts at the end adds lightness and texture. Serve with a handful of your favourite fresh herbs for an extra burst of freshness.

1 small iceberg lettuce
14 mussels, scrubbed and debearded
2 tablespoons light soy sauce
2 tablespoons shao hsing wine or dry sherry
1 teaspoon malt vinegar
1 teaspoon white sugar
½ teaspoon sesame oil
2 tablespoons peanut oil
5 cm × 2 cm knob (20 g) ginger, cut into fine julienne strips
1 garlic clove, finely diced
2 red shallots, halved and finely sliced
250 g firm-fleshed white fish fillet, roughly diced
100 g uncooked prawn meat, roughly diced
1 Chinese cabbage leaf, finely shredded
1 small carrot, cut into fine julienne strips
45 g (½ cup) bean sprouts
2 spring onions, finely sliced
1 tablespoon light soy sauce

Cut out the core of the lettuce. Soak the entire lettuce in cold water for 1 hour – this will make it easier to pull the leaves apart. Drain well and separate leaves. Cover and refrigerate until ready to serve.

Bring 125 ml (½ cup) water to the boil in a wok over high heat. Add mussels and cover. After 1–2 minutes, the mussels should start opening. As they begin to open, immediately remove them from wok with tongs and place in a bowl. You can use your tongs to tap on the shells to encourage them to open up, but discard any that have not opened after about 5 minutes. Drain water from wok and wipe clean with kitchen paper. Quickly rinse mussels under cold running water until cool enough to handle, then remove the mussel meat and set aside.

Combine soy sauce, wine or sherry, vinegar, sugar and sesame oil in a small bowl and set aside.

Heat peanut oil in a hot wok until the surface seems to shimmer slightly. Add ginger, garlic and shallot and stir-fry for 2 minutes or until caramelised, stirring regularly to make sure the garlic doesn't burn.

Add fish and prawns and stir-fry for 20 seconds. Add mussels and soy sauce mixture and cook for 30 seconds. Add cabbage, carrot, bean sprouts and spring onion and stir to combine. Remove from the heat.

Using a slotted spoon, remove seafood mixture from wok, draining well so that any juices are left in the wok. Serve in a bowl set on a large platter, drizzle over the soy sauce and accompany with lettuce-leaf cups. To eat, simply spoon seafood mixture into lettuce cups, roll up to enclose and eat with your fingers.

Serve as a starter for 4–6

STEAMED OCEAN TROUT WITH WAKAME AND CUCUMBER SALAD

While ocean trout is delicious roasted or grilled, or served as sashimi, I also like to lightly steam it – just for a few minutes, so it is still rare. With the addition of wakame, an incredibly nutritious seaweed, this salad is wholesome and refreshing.

1 × 450 g piece skinless ocean trout fillet, pin-boned and cut into 2 pieces
2 tablespoons vegetable oil, for brushing

MARINADE
5 cm × 2 cm knob (20 g) ginger
1 tablespoon light soy sauce
1 tablespoon honey
½ teaspoon sesame oil

WAKAME AND CUCUMBER SALAD
2 small cucumbers
1 teaspoon white sugar
1½ teaspoons salt flakes
25 g dried wakame seaweed
2 spring onions, cut into fine julienne strips
2 tablespoons apple cider vinegar
1 teaspoon light soy sauce

To make the marinade, finely grate ginger (a Microplane is ideal for this) directly into a large bowl, making sure all the juices go into the bowl. Add remaining marinade ingredients and stir to combine.

Add ocean trout to marinade and mix well. Refrigerate for 1 hour.

Meanwhile, make the wakame and cucumber salad. Halve cucumbers lengthways and scoop out the seeds using a teaspoon. Thinly slice the cucumbers into half-moons, place in a bowl, then sprinkle with sugar and 1 teaspoon salt and combine well with your hands. Refrigerate for 1 hour. Drain cucumber well, squeezing with your hands to remove any excess liquid.

Soak wakame in plenty of cold water for 10 minutes to rehydrate and soften. Drain well. (I like to use the nutrient-rich soaking water on my plants.) Using scissors, cut off the hard rib from the wakame strips and discard, then cut each strip into roughly bite-sized pieces for ease of eating. Set aside.

Bring a large saucepan or wok of water to the boil. Arrange ocean trout in a single layer in a shallow heatproof bowl that will fit inside a large steamer basket. Pour over the marinade, then place bowl inside steamer and cover with the lid. Position over the pan or wok of boiling water and steam for 4 minutes or until the fish is just slightly rare in the middle. Carefully remove bowl from steamer and transfer ocean trout to a chopping board, reserving the cooking juices. Flake the fish into large chunks and arrange on a serving platter.

Just as you're ready to serve, finish making the salad. Combine wakame, cucumber, spring onion, vinegar, soy sauce and remaining ½ teaspoon salt and toss well. Arrange ocean trout on top and serve immediately, drizzled with the reserved cooking juices.

Serve as part of a banquet for 4

GRILLED MARINATED SQUID

This is a really stunning dish to serve for a lunch or dinner party. If you can marinate the squid the night before, so much the better – and if you don't have a barbecue, simply cook it on your stovetop, preferably in a chargrill pan. Fresh squid should smell sweet with no trace of ammonia (which is sometimes used in the processing); it should be used soon after purchase and, because it readily absorbs water, it should never be left sitting in water or ice for long periods of time. If you're not inclined to clean the squid yourself, you can always buy ready-cleaned squid tubes – just make sure they're fresh and ask for small- to medium-sized ones. The honey and garlic in the marinade become mouth-wateringly caramelised as the squid is grilled, and a squeeze of lemon juice at the end balances out all those intense flavours.

---

350 g cleaned squid tubes
2 tablespoons vegetable oil, for brushing
pinch Sichuan Pepper and Salt (page 306)
1 lemon, cut into wedges

MARINADE

5 cm × 2 cm knob (20 g) ginger, finely diced
3 garlic cloves, finely diced
2 tablespoons light soy sauce
1½ tablespoons honey
1 teaspoon sesame oil
1 teaspoon dried chilli flakes

Combine marinade ingredients in a bowl and stir to combine well.

Add the whole squid tubes to the marinade and toss to coat well with your hands. Refrigerate for 30 minutes.

Preheat a chargrill pan or barbecue to high and brush lightly with oil. Place squid tubes on grill, reserving marinade, and cook for 2 minutes each side or until tender. Remove from grill and keep warm.

Pour reserved marinade into a small frying pan and cook over medium–high heat for 1 minute or until reduced by half.

Using a sharp knife, cut squid tubes into 1 cm thick slices and arrange on a serving platter. Pour over reduced marinade, garnish with Sichuan pepper and salt and serve with lemon wedges for squeezing over.

Serve as a starter for 4

CRAB AND ZUCCHINI CAKES WITH CHILLI–SOY DIPPING SAUCE

Because these cakes are made with a minimal amount of flour, they are extremely delicate and are best assembled just before you intend to cook them – though you can of course have all the ingredients prepared, chopped and drained beforehand. If you buy ready-picked crabmeat, it usually needs a good squeeze to remove any excess liquid; otherwise, your cakes will be soggy.

---

50 g (⅓ cup) plain flour
80 ml (⅓ cup) water
200 g freshly picked crabmeat
2 small zucchini (courgettes) – 250 g in total – cut into fine julienne strips
2 spring onions, white part only, finely sliced
1 stalk celery, cut into fine julienne strips
1 egg, lightly beaten
5 cm × 2 cm knob (20 g) ginger, cut into fine julienne strips
1 tablespoon light soy sauce
½ teaspoon white sugar
½ teaspoon sesame oil
½ teaspoon salt flakes
80 ml (⅓ cup) vegetable oil
80 ml (⅓ cup) Chilli–Soy Dipping Sauce (page 301), to serve (optional)

Combine flour and water in a small bowl to make a smooth batter.

Make the mixture for the cakes just before you're ready to cook them. Drain crabmeat well, squeezing with your hands to remove any excess liquid. Place in a large bowl, add all remaining ingredients except vegetable oil and chilli–soy dipping sauce and mix well with your hands. Add batter and stir through.

Heat vegetable oil in a large non-stick frying pan over medium–high heat. Working in batches, add small mounds (about 3 tablespoons) of mixture to pan and cook for 2 minutes, then carefully – they are very delicate – flip over using a spatula and cook the other side for 1 minute or until nicely golden and crisp. Remove from pan and drain on kitchen paper. Keep warm while you cook the rest.

Arrange cakes on a platter and serve immediately with a side dish of chilli–soy dipping sauce, if using.

Serve as a starter for 4 (makes 8)

POACHED LOBSTER WITH SPRING ONION–GINGER SAUCE

Definitely a dish for special occasions, this is incredibly simple to make, yet with very impressive results. I have found this method of poaching excellent for lobster: being very gentle, it truly respects the delicate flesh. As the lobster will continue to cook in its residual heat after you remove it from the pan, it is important to allow it to cool naturally for at least 30 minutes to complete the cooking process. Lobster cooked like this is of course suitable for serving in many other ways – with aioli, for example, or even in a decadent sandwich.

1 × 700–800 g live lobster

250 ml (1 cup) Spring Onion–Ginger Sauce (page 293)

Poach the lobster (page 166). Slice lobster tail into medallions, arrange on a serving platter and place reserved legs alongside.

Serve with spring onion–ginger sauce on the side.

Serves 2 as a main or 4 as part of a banquet

POACHING LOBSTER

❶ Place lobster in a plastic bag and leave in the freezer for 1 hour, where it will 'go to sleep'.

❷ Bring a large saucepan filled with water to the boil and carefully lower in the whole lobster, ensuring that it is completely submerged. Poach for 7 minutes, making sure the water does not boil again.

❸ Remove lobster with tongs. Drain on a tray or large plate and allow to cool for 30 minutes.

❼ Smash the legs with the flat blade of a large knife to crack the shells and set aside for garnish. (Freeze the head to make a seafood stock later, if you like.)

❽ Using kitchen scissors, cut along either side of the soft under-shell of the tail.

❹ Grab the lobster tail in one hand and the head in the other.

❺ Give the tail a good twist to pull the tail from the head.

❻ Break off the legs.

❾ Pull off the soft under-shell.

❿ Carefully remove the meat in one piece.

STEAMED LOBSTER WITH CHILLI SAUCE

You may have seen or tried the rather grand crab and lobster dishes in Chinese restaurants. Although this dish is equally grand in its appearance and impact, it's actually quite simple when taken step-by-step, and I encourage you to give it a go, so you can create an impressive Chinese banquet at home! First of all, I'd advise you to make the chilli sauce the day before. If you're worried about tangling with a lobster, ask your fishmonger to chop it up for you in the way required for this recipe (see over the page) – it will take them a matter of minutes. Just make sure you ask to keep the lobster 'mustard' from the head – this gives a richness and depth of flavour to the sauce that's to die for. Freshness is paramount when it comes to cooking seafood, so always try to buy your seafood on the same day you plan to cook it. Many Chinese restaurants would deep-fry the lobster for this recipe, but I prefer to steam it. Not only does this create less mess at home, but it is also a beautifully gentle way of cooking lobster. Finally, all that's left to do is combine the cooked lobster with the sauce and enjoy.

---

1 × 700–800 g live lobster
120 g (½ cup) Chilli Sauce (page 297)
1 tablespoon light soy sauce
1 teaspoon brown sugar
1 tablespoon peanut oil
5 cm × 1 cm knob (15 g) ginger, finely diced
3 tablespoons shao hsing wine or dry sherry
½ teaspoon sesame oil
1 teaspoon malt vinegar

First steam the lobster (page 170).

Combine chilli sauce, soy sauce and sugar in a small bowl, stirring to dissolve sugar. Heat peanut oil in a hot wok until the surface seems to shimmer slightly. Add ginger and stir-fry for 30 seconds.

Add wine or sherry and stir-fry for 30 seconds, then add chilli sauce mixture and stir-fry for 30 seconds or until sauce starts to caramelise.

Add lobster pieces and their cooking juices to the wok and toss well for 1 minute. Finally add sesame oil and vinegar, toss well, then transfer to a large platter and serve immediately.

Serves 2 as a main or 4 as part of a banquet

STEAMING LOBSTER

1 Place lobster in a plastic bag and leave in the freezer for 1 hour, where it will 'go to sleep'.

2 Remove lobster from freezer and place, belly-side down, on a chopping board. Using a tea towel to get a firm grip, hold tail down. Insert a sharp knife or cleaver between its eyes.

5 Chop each half into quarters.

6 Do not be tempted to rinse – you want to keep the 'mustard' for added flavour.

❸ Pressing down on the flat of the knife with the heel of your hand, cut the lobster in half lengthways.

❹ Ease the two halves of the lobster apart.

❼ Place lobster pieces in a shallow heatproof bowl that will fit inside a large steamer basket. Bring a large saucepan or wok of water to the boil. Place bowl inside steamer and cover with the lid. Position over pan or wok of boiling water and steam for about 6 minutes or until cooked.

❽ Check to see if the lobster is cooked: the flesh should be white; if it is still translucent, cook for another minute or so.

EGGS

CRISPY-SKIN EGGS, CARAMELISED CHICKEN AND PICKLES

At first glance, this dish may appear somewhat fiddly, but don't be put off: both the pickles are made several days beforehand, so they will be ready to go. You can always get your butcher to chop up the chicken wings for you, and you could steam them the day before if you need to, then simply deep-fry them before serving. This is a scrumptious, finger-licking sort of a dish that is just bursting with texture and flavour.

4 free-range chicken wings, each cut into 3 pieces
4 free-range eggs, at room temperature
185 g (1 cup) lightly packed brown sugar
500 ml (2 cups) vegetable oil
3 tablespoons cornflour
3 tablespoons fish sauce
3 small iceberg lettuce leaves
juice of 1 lime
65 g (½ cup) Pickled Cucumber (page 250)
3 halves each red and green Pickled Chillies (page 257)
1 bird's eye chilli from Pickled Chillies (page 257), thinly sliced

Bring a large saucepan or wok of water to the boil. Place chicken pieces in a shallow heatproof bowl that will fit inside a steamer basket. Place bowl inside steamer and cover with the lid. Position over the pan or wok of boiling water and steam for about 10 minutes or until chicken is cooked. Remove chicken and drain well on kitchen paper.

Meanwhile, place eggs in a small saucepan of boiling water and cook for 4 minutes (or 5 minutes if using eggs straight from the fridge). Remove eggs using a slotted spoon and refresh under cold running water. Carefully peel eggs and drain well on kitchen paper.

Place sugar and 250 ml (1 cup) water in a large frying pan and bring to the boil, stirring to dissolve sugar. Cook for 6 minutes or until caramelised – the sauce will bubble up and become sticky. Remove caramel sauce from heat and set aside.

Heat oil in a hot wok until the surface seems to shimmer slightly (190°C). Using a slotted spoon, carefully lower eggs into hot oil and deep-fry for about 2 minutes each side or until golden and crisp all over – the yolks should still be soft inside. Remove from wok with a slotted spoon and drain on kitchen paper.

Lightly dust chicken pieces in cornflour, shaking off any excess, then deep-fry in the same oil as the eggs – you will need to do this in two batches. Cook each batch for 1 minute each side or until golden and crisp. Remove using tongs and drain on kitchen paper.

Return caramel sauce to medium–high heat, add chicken pieces and fish sauce, stir to coat well, then cook for 2 minutes.

Arrange lettuce on a plate and place caramelised chicken on top, leaving sauce in pan. Using your hands, gently break eggs in half and arrange around chicken. Squeeze lime juice into pan, then spoon sauce over chicken. Serve with side dishes of pickled cucumber and chilli.

Serve as a starter for 4 or as part of a banquet for 4

HOME-STYLE FRIED EGGS WITH ROASTED PORK

My Uncle Jimmy's mother, dear Mrs Jang, didn't know she was creating a legendary dish some 35 years ago, when she used to serve a version of this to all of us Kwong kids for lunch. Try to use organic eggs, if possible – you'll really notice the difference in flavour and texture. If you don't have the time to make Roasted Pork Shoulder with Miso and Honey (page 119), by all means substitute BBQ pork bought from Chinatown. Served with steamed rice, this makes a delicious and substantial one-dish meal.

---

2 tablespoons Caramel Spiced Soy Sauce (page 294)
250 g roasted pork, warm or at room temperature, thinly sliced
375 ml (1½ cups) vegetable oil
6 free-range eggs
pinch freshly ground white pepper
2 spring onions, finely sliced
1 small red chilli, finely sliced

First make the caramel spiced soy sauce. Remove from heat and leave to infuse for 1 hour, then discard cinnamon and star anise. Gently reheat sauce in a small saucepan, then add roasted pork to warm through. Keep warm until ready to serve.

Heat oil in a hot wok until the surface seems to shimmer slightly.

Crack eggs into a bowl, then pour into hot oil – the eggs will billow up. Cook for 1 minute without stirring. Reduce heat to medium and cook for a further 30 seconds.

Carefully slide a spatula under the eggs and lift up while pouring off the oil. Discard oil. Replace eggs in pan and cook for a further minute, allowing the underside of the eggs to become firm and crisp – the yolks should still be a little runny. If, like me, you prefer your yolks quite gooey, then only cook the eggs for a further 10–30 seconds at this point.

Gently remove eggs from wok and drain off any excess oil before easing onto a plate. Garnish with spring onion and chilli and serve with the roasted pork and sauce in a bowl on the side.

Serve as a starter for 4 or as a meal with steamed rice for 2

CRAB OMELETTE WITH PICKLED WHITE RADISH AND FRESH HERBS

With its combination of crab, shallots, radish and vinegar, this dish takes its inspiration from France, but I've given it an Asian twist. I love the subtle and soft colours of this omelette, the secret to which lies in finding super-fresh crabmeat and the best-quality eggs.

---

200 g (1 cup) picked fresh crabmeat
2 red shallots, halved and thinly sliced
½ bunch dill, leaves picked
½ bunch coriander, leaves picked
2 teaspoons malt vinegar
6 free-range eggs
2 tablespoons vegetable oil

QUICK PICKLED WHITE RADISH
250 g white radish (daikon) – about ⅓ small one
1 teaspoon salt flakes
1 teaspoon white sugar

To make the quick pickled white radish, peel and slice the radish into thin rounds, then slice rounds to make mini-matchsticks. Place radish, salt and sugar in a bowl and combine well with your hands. Refrigerate for 1 hour. Drain liquid from radish, squeezing with your hands to remove any excess liquid.

Combine radish with crabmeat, shallot, herbs and vinegar and toss with your hands to distribute ingredients evenly.

Crack eggs into a bowl and beat lightly with a fork until just combined.

Heat oil in a wok or 28 cm non-stick frying pan until the surface seems to shimmer slightly. Pour in beaten egg and leave to cook, without stirring, on the base of the wok or pan for 30 seconds.

Using a spatula, fold beaten egg over onto itself and leave to cook for another 30 seconds.

Add crabmeat filling, fold omelette over and leave for 20 seconds or until almost set.

Fold omelette over again and leave for another 20 seconds before lifting omelette onto a serving platter. Serve immediately.

Serve as a starter for 2–4

STIR-FRIED OMELETTE WITH SNOW PEAS, HERBS AND BEAN SPROUTS

Alive with colourful, vibrant and wholesome ingredients, this omelette is perfect for vegetarians. Make sure you slice the vegetables up finely – and if you wish to add vegetables that need cooking (beans, zucchini, cauliflower, broccoli and the like), remember you'll need to trim, slice and cook them before you start making the omelette. Think of this as a big fresh salad encased in an omelette!

6 free-range eggs
2 tablespoons vegetable oil
180 ml (¾ cup) Spring Onion–Chilli Sauce (page 294), to serve

OMELETTE FILLING

100 g snow peas, trimmed and cut into fine julienne strips
½ carrot, cut into fine julienne strips
90 g (1 cup) bean sprouts
½ bunch coriander, leaves picked
½ bunch mint, leaves picked
½ bunch dill, leaves picked

Crack eggs into a bowl and beat lightly with a fork until just combined.

Combine omelette filling ingredients in a large bowl.

Heat oil in a wok or 28 cm non-stick frying pan until the surface seems to shimmer slightly. Pour in beaten egg and leave to cook, without stirring, on base of wok or pan for 30 seconds.

Using a spatula, fold beaten egg over onto itself and leave to cook for another 30 seconds.

Add filling, fold omelette over and leave for 20 seconds or until almost set.

Fold omelette over again and leave for another 20 seconds before lifting omelette onto a serving platter. Serve with spring onion–chilli sauce on the side for dipping.

Serve as a starter for 2–4

OMELETTE WITH GLASS NOODLES AND TOMATO AND ZUCCHINI SAUCE

I really like the slippery texture of glass noodles. In this recipe I stir them into beaten egg, which is then made into an omelette, and dressed with a fresh tomato and zucchini sauce. The longer cooking time for this omelette is needed to ensure that the glass noodles in the mixture are heated through.

50 g glass (bean thread) noodles
6 free-range eggs
2 red shallots, thinly sliced
2 tablespoons vegetable oil

TOMATO AND ZUCCHINI SAUCE
1 tablespoon light soy sauce
1 teaspoon malt vinegar
1 teaspoon brown sugar
½ teaspoon sesame oil
2 tablespoons peanut oil
5 cm × 3 cm knob (25 g) ginger, finely diced
2 tomatoes, cut into wedges
2 tablespoons shao hsing wine or dry sherry
1 zucchini (courgette), cut into fine julienne strips

Soak noodles in hot tap water for 15 minutes. Drain well.

Crack eggs into a bowl and beat lightly with a fork until just combined. Stir in shallot and noodles.

To make the tomato and zucchini sauce, combine soy sauce, vinegar, sugar and sesame oil in a small bowl. Heat peanut oil in a frying pan over medium–high heat. Add ginger and tomato and cook, stirring occasionally, for 1 minute. Add wine or sherry and cook for 30 seconds. Add soy sauce mixture and cook for 30 seconds. Remove from heat and keep warm until ready to serve.

Heat vegetable oil in a wok or 28 cm non-stick frying pan until the surface seems to shimmer slightly. Pour in egg mixture and leave to cook on base of wok or pan, without stirring, for 2 minutes or until centre is just set. Using a spatula, flip omelette over and cook for another 10 seconds.

Slide omelette onto a platter and fold in half. Briefly reheat sauce, if necessary, then stir in zucchini. Spoon the tomato and zucchini over the omelette, along with a little of the sauce. Serve immediately.

Serve as a starter for 2–4

DEEP-FRIED SOFT-BOILED EGGS WITH ICEBERG LETTUCE AND CHILLI SALT

A really quick and simple recipe that makes for a great, tasty yet substantial snack – it's crunchy, sour, gooey, silky, salty and spicy all at once.

8 free-range eggs, at room temperature
vegetable oil, for deep-frying
½ iceberg lettuce, shredded
2 spring onions, cut into fine julienne strips
½ teaspoon Chilli Salt (page 305)

QUICK PICKLED CUCUMBER
1 small cucumber, trimmed
½ teaspoon salt flakes
½ teaspoon white sugar
juice of 1 lemon
½ teaspoon fish sauce

Place eggs in a small saucepan of boiling water and cook for 4 minutes (or 5 minutes if using eggs straight from the fridge). Remove eggs using a slotted spoon and refresh under cold running water. Carefully peel eggs (if they are very fresh, it may be easier to do this in a bowl of cold water), then drain well on kitchen paper.

Meanwhile, make the quick pickled cucumber. Halve cucumber lengthways, scoop out and discard seeds, then cut into thin slices on the diagonal. Place in a bowl with salt and sugar and combine well with your hands. Refrigerate for 15 minutes.

Pour enough oil for deep-frying into a wok and heat until the surface seems to shimmer slightly (190°C). Using a slotted spoon, carefully lower eggs into hot oil and deep-fry for about 2 minutes each side or until golden and crisp all over. The eggs should still be soft in the centre. Remove from wok with a slotted spoon and drain on kitchen paper.

Drain liquid from pickled cucumber, squeezing well with your hands, then toss with lemon juice and fish sauce.

To make the salad, combine pickled cucumber with lettuce and spring onion.

Using a sharp knife, cut eggs in half and serve with the salad. Garnish with chilli salt to serve.

Serve as part of a banquet for 8

STEAMED SAVOURY PORK CUSTARD

This is one of the rustic dishes my mum used to whip up on weeknights when she was pressed for time and lacked the wherewithal to cook her usual five-dish Chinese meal for us all. This is comfort food at its best: you simply stir minced pork into beaten egg, season it, steam it and then serve it with steamed rice – and fresh chilli, if you like.

---

4 free-range eggs, at room temperature
3 tablespoons shao hsing wine or dry sherry
150 g minced pork belly
5 cm × 1 cm knob (15 g) ginger, cut into fine julienne strips
2 spring onions, thinly sliced
¼ bunch coriander, stems thinly sliced and leaves picked
2 Braised Chinese Mushrooms (page 220), drained and thinly sliced, or 2 fresh shiitake mushrooms, stems removed and caps thinly sliced
1 tablespoon light soy sauce
½ teaspoon sesame oil
Steamed Rice (page 262), to serve

Bring a large saucepan or wok of water to the boil.

Crack eggs into a large bowl, add wine or sherry and lightly beat. Add pork, ginger, spring onion, coriander stems and mushrooms, then stir to combine well. Pour mixture into a 20 cm diameter (500 ml capacity) heatproof bowl that will fit inside a large steamer basket – the egg mixture should be no more than 4 cm deep in the bowl, otherwise it may not set properly.

Place bowl inside steamer and cover with the lid. Position over the pan or wok of boiling water and steam for about 18 minutes or until egg is set.

Remove from steamer, drizzle with combined soy sauce and sesame oil and garnish with coriander leaves. Serve immediately with steamed rice.

Serve with steamed rice as a meal for 2

STEAMED CRAB CUSTARD WITH ENOKI MUSHROOMS

A very delicate dish with a super-smooth, silky texture that's achieved by straining the beaten egg, then steaming it over a very gentle heat. To help the custard to cook evenly, steam it in a shallow bowl with a flat base and relatively straight sides, so the egg mixture will be a uniform depth throughout.

2 eggs, at room temperature
250 ml (1 cup) chicken stock or water, at room temperature
150 g freshly picked crabmeat, drained and squeezed dry
2 red shallots, finely sliced
50 g enoki mushrooms (½ packet), bases trimmed and gently separated
5 cm × 1 cm knob (15 g) ginger, cut into fine julienne strips
1 teaspoon light soy sauce
Steamed Rice (page 262), to serve

Bring a large saucepan or wok of water to the boil.

Meanwhile, crack eggs into a bowl and gently beat with a fork in one direction only (you don't want to incorporate too much air into the eggs). Strain beaten egg through a coarse sieve into a jug or bowl and discard any thick bits of egg white in sieve.

Gently stir all remaining ingredients except soy sauce and rice into strained egg. Pour into a 20 cm diameter (500 ml capacity) heatproof bowl that will fit inside a large steamer basket – the egg mixture should be no more than 4 cm deep in the bowl, otherwise it may not set properly.

Place bowl inside steamer, cover with the lid and position over the pan or wok of boiling water. Immediately reduce heat to a gentle simmer and steam for 20–25 minutes or until egg is just set – there should still be a slight wobble in the centre.

Remove bowl from steamer and set aside for 5 minutes. The custard will continue to cook and set during this time. Drizzle with soy sauce and serve with rice.

Serve with steamed rice as a meal for 2

VEGETABLES AND TOFU

SUNG CHOI BAO OF VEGETABLES

A wonderful dish for vegetarians, with endless variations: you could add corn kernels, freshly shaved from the cob, at the same time as the beans and celery; you could include any number of fresh herbs; or you could substitute any kind of fresh mushrooms for the braised Chinese mushrooms. Just make sure your iceberg lettuce cups are well-chilled and super-crispy for maximum effect.

---

1 small iceberg lettuce
2 tablespoons light soy sauce
1 tablespoon malt vinegar
1 teaspoon brown sugar
½ teaspoon sesame oil
2 tablespoons peanut oil
5 cm × 2 cm knob (20 g) ginger, roughly diced
2 garlic cloves, roughly diced
½ small red onion, finely sliced
4 Braised Chinese Mushrooms (page 220), stems removed and finely sliced
80 g green beans, trimmed and finely sliced
2 sticks celery, trimmed and finely diced
2 tablespoons shao hsing wine or dry sherry
1 Chinese cabbage leaf, finely shredded
1 small carrot, cut into fine julienne strips
1 small cucumber, cut into fine julienne strips
45 g (½ cup) bean sprouts
½ bunch garlic chives, cut into 5 cm lengths
sliced large red chilli, to serve (optional)

Cut out and discard the core of the lettuce, then soak the entire lettuce in cold water for 1 hour (this will make it easier to pull apart the leaves). Drain well and separate leaves. Cover and refrigerate until ready to serve.

Combine soy sauce, vinegar, sugar and sesame oil in a small bowl and set aside.

Heat peanut oil in a hot wok until the surface seems to shimmer slightly. Add ginger, garlic, onion and mushrooms and stir-fry for 1 minute.

Add beans and celery and stir-fry for 1 minute. Add wine or sherry and cook for 30 seconds.

Add soy sauce mixture and stir-fry for 2 minutes or until sauce is slightly thickened.

Add cabbage, carrot, cucumber, bean sprouts and garlic chives and stir to combine. Remove from the heat.

Using a slotted spoon, remove vegetable mixture from wok, draining well so that any juices are left in the wok. Serve in a bowl set on a large platter, accompanied with lettuce-leaf cups. To eat, simply spoon vegetable mixture into lettuce cups, roll up to enclose and eat with your fingers. Serve with sliced chilli, if you like.

Serve as a starter for 4–6

VEGETARIAN SPRING ROLLS

Tofu or bean curd comes in many forms and can be prepared and cooked in various ways. For my spring rolls I like to use dried bean-curd skins, which are available in Chinatown. The trimming of the bean-curd skins is a bit fiddly, but the fresh, light texture it lends the rolls make it worth the effort. The noodle filling is full of interesting textures and aromatics. These spring rolls are best eaten immediately, dipped in sweet chilli sauce.

2 packets (500 g) dried bean curd skin
1 free-range egg, lightly beaten
vegetable oil, for deep-frying
125 ml (½ cup) Sweet Chilli Sauce (page 297)

FILLING

50 g glass (bean thread) noodles
2 free-range eggs
2 tablespoons vegetable oil
½ small carrot, cut into fine julienne strips
½ small cucumber, cut into fine julienne strips
1 spring onion, cut into fine julienne strips
½ bunch mint, leaves picked
½ bunch coriander, leaves picked
50 g fresh black cloud ear fungus (½ packet), cores removed, finely sliced
45 g (½ cup) bean sprouts

To make the filling, soak noodles in hot tap water for 15 minutes. Drain thoroughly and, using scissors, cut noodles into small lengths. Place in a large bowl and set aside.

Crack eggs into a bowl and lightly beat. Heat 1 tablespoon oil in a non-stick frying pan over medium–high heat until the surface seems to shimmer slightly. Pour in half of the beaten egg and tilt pan to spread mixture evenly over base and make an 'egg crepe'. Cook for 1 minute, without disturbing – the egg will bubble up and become lightly golden underneath. Carefully slide egg crepe onto a plate lined with kitchen paper to drain. Wipe out pan, add another tablespoon of oil and remaining beaten egg and repeat process. When crepes have cooled slightly, roll each one up individually and cut into 3 mm thick slices.

Add egg to noodles with remaining filling ingredients and mix thoroughly. Set aside.

Next, make and cook the spring rolls (page 196).

Using a sharp knife, cut each roll in half on the diagonal. Serve immediately, with sweet chilli sauce for dipping.

Serve as a starter for 4

MAKING SPRING ROLLS

❶ Cut bean curd skins into 18 cm square wrappers – you will need about 8–10 wrappers. Cover wrappers with a damp tea towel until needed, to keep them malleable and prevent them drying out.

❷ Place a wrapper on a work surface with one of the corners facing you (keep the other wrappers covered still). Place ½ cup of filling in middle of wrapper.

❺ Fold in each side, and continue rolling to make a cigar shape about 10 cm long and 3 cm in diameter.

❻ To seal the spring roll, dab along the open flap with beaten egg and press to seal.

❸ Arrange the filling into a log diagonally across the wrapper.

❹ Starting at the corner nearest to you, roll the wrapper over the filling very tightly.

❺ As you finish making each spring roll, place it seam-side down on a tray. Cover with a damp tea towel while you make the other rolls.

❻ Pour enough oil for deep-frying into a wok and heat until the surface seems to shimmer (190°C). Working in batches, deep-fry the spring rolls for 30 seconds each side or until lightly golden and puffed up. Remove spring rolls using tongs and drain on kitchen paper.

STIR-FRIED CHINESE CABBAGE WITH TOFU AND GLASS NOODLES

Five-spice pressed tofu is excellent for stir-frying because it is robust and firm – unlike silken tofu, which is much better suited to steaming. I love this combination of ingredients: because the tofu has been slow-braised with soy sauce and star anise, it has a beautiful caramel colour and flavour, and contrasts well with the slippery glass noodles, velvety cloud ear fungus and sweet, crisp Chinese cabbage. If you're not cooking for vegetarians, you could always add Tea-Smoked Oysters (page 132) to this – bring them to room temperature and arrange on top just before serving.

- 100 g glass (bean thread) noodles
- 3 tablespoons light soy sauce
- 1 tablespoon malt vinegar
- 1 tablespoon brown sugar
- ½ teaspoon sesame oil
- 2 tablespoons peanut oil
- 5 cm × 2 cm knob (20 g) ginger, finely sliced
- 6 small Braised Chinese Mushrooms (page 220), left whole
- 110 g five-spice pressed tofu (½ packet), finely sliced
- 3 tablespoons shao hsing wine or dry sherry
- 2 garlic cloves, crushed
- 2 Chinese cabbage leaves, thickly sliced on the diagonal
- 100 g fresh black cloud ear fungus (1 packet), cores removed, roughly torn
- 2 spring onions, cut into 7 cm lengths

Soak noodles in hot tap water for 15 minutes. Drain well and, using kitchen scissors, roughly cut into manageable lengths.

Combine soy sauce, vinegar, sugar and sesame oil in a small bowl and set aside.

Heat peanut oil in a hot wok until the surface seems to shimmer slightly. Add ginger, mushrooms and tofu and cook, stirring occasionally, for 2 minutes or until tofu is lightly golden.

Add wine or sherry and cook for 30 seconds. Add garlic, cabbage and black cloud ear fungus and stir-fry for 1 minute.

Add soy sauce mixture, noodles and spring onion and stir-fry for 2 minutes or until noodles are heated through. Serve immediately.

Serve as part of a banquet for 4–6

The remaining tofu can be stored in the fridge for up to a week.

STIR-FRIED KING BROWN AND CHINESE MUSHROOMS WITH CELERY

King brown mushrooms are absolutely stunning! When their thick, bulbous stems are cut into fine slices then stir-fried, they become firm yet silky, almost like abalone. For a change, you could stir through some Pickled Celery (page 257) right at the end – start with 3 or 4 tablespoons, adding more to taste.

3 teaspoons light soy sauce
1 teaspoon malt vinegar
1 teaspoon brown sugar
½ teaspoon sesame oil
2 tablespoons peanut oil
5 cm × 2 cm knob (20 g) ginger, finely sliced
2 garlic cloves, crushed
250 g king brown mushrooms, cut into 5 mm thick slices
6 Braised Chinese Mushrooms (page 220), halved on the diagonal
2 small sticks celery, cut into 5 mm thick slices on the diagonal
3 tablespoons shao hsing wine or dry sherry

Combine soy sauce, vinegar, sugar and sesame oil in a small bowl and set aside.

Heat peanut oil in a hot wok until the surface seems to shimmer slightly. Add ginger and garlic and stir-fry for 10 seconds.

Add all of the mushrooms and stir-fry for 2½ minutes or until lightly golden and just tender.

Add celery and cook for 10 seconds. Add wine or sherry and cook for 1 minute.

Add soy sauce mixture and stir-fry for 30 seconds, tossing to coat everything in the sauce. Serve immediately.

Serve as part of a banquet for 4

STIR-FRIED POTATO WITH CHILLI SAUCE AND BLACK BEANS

The Chinese have some original ways with potatoes. This stir-fry makes a welcome change from roasted, fried, baked or mashed – the starchiness of potato is a great foil for the big, bold flavours of chilli and salted black beans.

- 2 tablespoons Chilli Sauce (page 297)
- 1½ tablespoons light soy sauce
- 1 teaspoon malt vinegar
- 1 teaspoon brown sugar
- ½ teaspoon sesame oil
- 2 tablespoons peanut oil
- 3 large red chillies, seeds removed, halved
- 3 small potatoes – about 650 g in total – peeled, halved and cut into 5 mm thick slices
- 3 red shallots, cut into eighths
- 2 tablespoons shao hsing wine or dry sherry
- 2 teaspoons salted black beans
- pinch Sichuan Pepper and Salt (page 306) – optional

Combine chilli sauce, soy sauce, vinegar, sugar and sesame oil with 2 tablespoons water in a small bowl and set aside.

Heat peanut oil in a hot wok until the surface seems to shimmer slightly. Add halved chillies and cook for 30 seconds each side to 'blister' and slightly blacken. Remove with tongs and drain on kitchen paper. Reserve oil in wok.

Add potato to wok and cook for 2 minutes on each side or until lightly golden. Turn over occasionally using a spatula to get a good colour on both sides.

Add shallot to wok, toss to combine and cook for 2 minutes. Add wine or sherry and cook for 10 seconds. Add black beans and stir-fry for 1 minute, stirring regularly to make sure the black beans don't burn and become bitter.

Add chilli sauce mixture and cook for 3 minutes or until potato is just tender. Transfer to a plate, garnish with blistered chillies and sprinkle over Sichuan pepper and salt, if desired.

Serve as part of a banquet for 4–6

STIR-FRIED ICEBERG LETTUCE WITH XO SAUCE

The Chinese generally cook iceberg lettuce, rather than serving it raw in salads. When stir-fried in this recipe, the meaty iceberg lettuce leaves wilt slightly, absorbing all the intense flavours of the XO sauce – it's incredibly simple, yet so tasty. If you're after a completely vegetarian dish, try making this with Chilli Sauce (page 297) instead of XO.

1 iceberg lettuce
5 tablespoons XO Sauce (page 298)
1½ tablespoons light soy sauce
1 teaspoon white sugar
1 tablespoon peanut oil
5 cm × 2 cm knob (20 g) ginger, finely sliced
3 tablespoons shao hsing wine or dry sherry
1 teaspoon malt vinegar
½ teaspoon sesame oil
pinch Sichuan Pepper and Salt (page 306)

Remove and discard outer leaves and core of lettuce. Roughly chop lettuce into 9 cm × 5 cm pieces and separate leaves into a bowl (there's no need to rinse them).

Combine XO sauce, soy sauce and sugar in a small bowl and set aside.

Heat peanut oil in a hot wok until the surface seems to shimmer slightly. Add ginger and stir-fry for 30 seconds or until fragrant. Carefully add wine or sherry – it may spit – and cook for 30 seconds.

Add XO sauce mixture and cook, stirring occasionally, for 30 seconds to caramelise. Add 1 tablespoon water and cook for another 30 seconds.

Next, add lettuce and toss to coat for 1 minute. Add vinegar and sesame oil and stir-fry, tossing the lettuce often, for 1 minute or until lettuce has slightly wilted.

Transfer to a serving plate, sprinkle over Sichuan pepper and salt and serve immediately.

Serves as a side dish as part of a banquet for 4–6

STIR-FRIED BRUSSELS SPROUTS AND CAULIFLOWER WITH BLACK SESAME SEEDS

During the winter months, I often cook brussels sprouts and cauliflower. They go very well with Chinese flavours such as ginger, garlic and soy sauce. I like a slight crunch to my vegetables, hence the timing in this recipe; if you prefer yours softer, by all means cook them for a little longer. This recipe would also be great with fine slivers of lup cheong sausage – simply add them to the stir-fry at the same time as the ginger and spring onion.

2 tablespoons light soy sauce
1 tablespoon malt vinegar
1 tablespoon brown sugar
1 teaspoon sesame oil
2 tablespoons peanut oil
5 cm × 2 cm knob (20 g) ginger, finely sliced
3 red shallots, cut into eighths
3 tablespoons shao hsing wine or dry sherry
250 g brussels sprouts, halved
300 g cauliflower (about ⅓ small one), cut into small florets
2 garlic cloves, finely sliced
1 tablespoon black sesame seeds

Combine soy sauce, vinegar, sugar and sesame oil in a small bowl and set aside.

Heat peanut oil in a hot wok until the surface seems to shimmer slightly. Add ginger and shallot and stir-fry for 2 minutes or until the shallot begins to caramelise. Add wine or sherry and stir-fry for 30 seconds.

Add brussels sprouts, cauliflower and garlic and stir-fry for 2 minutes.

Add soy sauce mixture, toss to coat vegetables, then cover and cook for 4–6 minutes or until cauliflower and brussels sprouts are just tender.

Sprinkle over sesame seeds and toss well. Serve immediately.

Serve as part of a banquet for 4

CHINESE MUSHROOMS STUFFED WITH PRAWNS, LUP CHEONG SAUSAGE AND CORIANDER

The lup cheong sausage makes a very tasty addition to this stuffing, as it combines well with the rich, meaty Chinese mushrooms. If you prefer not to eat meat, you could substitute the lup cheong with fillet of snapper, bream or blue eye, or even with scallops.

12 large Braised Chinese Mushrooms (page 220)

STUFFING

1 lup cheong sausage, finely diced
10 uncooked king prawns, peeled, deveined and chopped (about 250 g prawn meat)
5 cm × 1 cm knob (15 g) ginger, finely diced
½ bunch coriander, stems and roots only, washed and finely chopped
1 tablespoon light soy sauce
1 tablespoon shao hsing wine or dry sherry
½ teaspoon white sugar
½ teaspoon sesame oil

Bring a large saucepan or wok of water to the boil.

Place all of the stuffing ingredients in a bowl and combine well using your hands.

Place the mushrooms, cap-side down, on a plate and place 1 tablespoon prawn stuffing inside each one, packing the mixture down firmly with your fingers.

Arrange the stuffed mushrooms in a single layer on a heatproof plate that will fit inside a large steamer basket. Place bowl inside steamer and cover with the lid. Position over the pan or wok of boiling water and steam for about 8 minutes or until prawn stuffing is cooked.

Remove bowl from steamer and serve the stuffed mushrooms immediately.

Serve as part of a banquet for 4–6

CRISPY EGGPLANT WITH SESAME DRESSING

Eggplant features in the Chinese kitchen in many guises: stir-fried, braised, steamed, pickled, grilled, smoked and roasted. In this recipe it is deep-fried then served with a rich, sesame dressing made from sesame paste. You could also serve this crispy eggplant with a bowl of Chilli Sauce (page 297) or XO Sauce (page 298) on the side.

3–4 small eggplants (aubergines) – about 700 g in total – quartered lengthways
2 teaspoons salt flakes
vegetable oil, for deep-frying
½ tablespoon roasted sesame seeds

SESAME DRESSING
2 tablespoons sesame paste (unhulled tahini)
1 tablespoon sesame oil
1 tablespoon light soy sauce
2 teaspoons malt vinegar
1–2 tablespoons water

To make the sesame dressing, place sesame paste, sesame oil and soy sauce in a bowl and whisk well to combine. Whisk in vinegar, then whisk in enough water to give a smooth, runny consistency. Set aside until required (the dressing can be stored in an airtight container in the refrigerator for up to 2 days).

Place eggplant on a tray, sprinkle all over with the salt and set aside for 45 minutes. Pat thoroughly dry with kitchen paper to remove the bitter juices that will have leached out.

Pour enough oil for deep-frying into a wok and heat until the surface seems to shimmer slightly (190°C). Add eggplant in batches and deep-fry for 4–6 minutes or until golden. Remove with a slotted spoon and drain on kitchen paper.

Arrange eggplant on a platter, drizzle with sesame dressing and garnish with sesame seeds.

Serve as part of a banquet for 4

STIR-FRIED ZUCCHINI FLOWERS AND CAULIFLOWER WITH GARLIC AND SOY SAUCE

A simple stir-fry that celebrates fresh, seasonal produce. If zucchini flowers are unavailable, you can use 200 g zucchini, trimmed and cut into batons – or feel free to use your favourite vegetables instead.

- 2 tablespoons light soy sauce
- 1 tablespoon malt vinegar
- 1 teaspoon brown sugar
- ½ teaspoon sesame oil
- 2 tablespoons peanut oil
- 5 cm × 2 cm knob (20 g) ginger, finely sliced
- 4 garlic cloves, crushed
- 200 g cauliflower (about ⅓ medium one), cut into small florets
- 200 g zucchini (courgette) flowers, halved lengthways
- 2 tablespoons shao hsing wine or dry sherry

Combine soy sauce, vinegar, sugar and sesame oil in a small bowl.

Heat peanut oil in a hot wok until the surface seems to shimmer slightly. Add ginger, garlic and cauliflower and stir-fry for 2 minutes.

Add zucchini flowers and stir-fry for 30 seconds. Add wine or sherry and cook for 30 seconds.

Add soy sauce mixture, toss to coat vegetables, then cover and cook for 2 minutes or until zucchini flowers and cauliflower are just tender. Serve immediately.

Serve as part of a banquet for 4–6

STIR-FRIED CORN, PEAS, CHINESE MUSHROOMS AND POTATO

This pleasingly rustic vegetarian dish uses a variety of vegetables. You could use fresh shiitake mushrooms instead of braised Chinese mushrooms: just slice thinly and add to the wok at the same time as the corn and potato. Somewhat perversely, I like eating corn kernels and peas with chopsticks – although progress can be slow, it makes you savour every single mouthful, and there is a certain triumphant feeling when you manage to get the pea or kernel between your chopsticks!

2¼ tablespoons light soy sauce
1 tablespoon malt vinegar
2 teaspoons brown sugar
½ teaspoon sesame oil
150 g (1 cup) fresh or frozen green peas (about 400 g peas in pods)
2 tablespoons peanut oil
5 cm × 2 cm knob (20 g) ginger, finely diced
½ small red onion, halved and finely sliced
5 Braised Chinese Mushrooms (page 220), finely sliced
2 small corn cobs, kernels removed – to yield 250 g (1¼ cups) corn kernels
1 potato (350 g), peeled and cut into fine julienne strips
3 tablespoons shao hsing wine or sherry

Combine soy sauce, vinegar, sugar and sesame oil in a small bowl and set aside.

Blanch peas in boiling water for 1 minute. Drain, refresh under cold running water and set aside.

Heat peanut oil in a hot wok until the surface seems to shimmer slightly. Add ginger, onion and mushrooms and stir-fry for 2 minutes or until onion is soft and translucent.

Add corn and potato and stir-fry 2 minutes. Add peas and cook for 30 seconds. Next, add wine or sherry and cook for 30 seconds.

Add soy sauce mixture and cook for 2 minutes or until vegetables are just tender. Serve immediately.

Serve as part of a banquet for 4–6

CRISPY TOFU WITH FISH STUFFING

I like to make the stuffing from soft, delicate fish, so it won't easily break through the walls of the tofu. Alternatively, you could use prawn meat to stuff the tofu, then serve it with Sweet Chilli Sauce (page 297).

1 × 500 g packet (12 squares) firm tofu
160 ml (⅔ cup) vegetable oil
60 g (½ cup) cornflour
pinch Sichuan Pepper and Salt (page 306)
250 ml (1 cup) Chilli–Soy Dipping Sauce (page 301), to serve

STUFFING
200 g white-fleshed fish fillet, such as snapper, finely diced
5 cm × 2 cm knob (20 g) ginger, finely diced
1 spring onion, finely sliced
½ bunch coriander, stem and roots only, washed and finely sliced
1 tablespoon light soy sauce
1 tablespoon shao hsing wine or dry sherry
½ teaspoon white sugar
½ teaspoon sesame oil

To make the stuffing, place all of the ingredients in a bowl and combine well with your hands.

Remove tofu from the packet and drain well. Pat dry with kitchen paper. It's important to make sure the tofu is thoroughly dry otherwise it will spit when fried. Cut each tofu square in half on the diagonal to make 2 triangles. Working with one triangle at a time, hold a triangle in one hand with the cut side facing you. Using a teaspoon, hollow out the centre of the cut side to make a deep pocket, but make sure you don't break the walls of the triangle. Discard the tofu scraps and hollow out the remaining triangles.

Bring a large saucepan or wok of water to the boil.

Fill each tofu triangle with 1 teaspoon of the fish stuffing, pressing the mixture down firmly with the back of the spoon. Place stuffed tofu in a single layer on 2 heatproof plates that will fit inside a large steamer basket. Place the first plate inside the steamer and cover with the lid. Position over the pan or wok of boiling water and steam for about 4 minutes or until fish stuffing is cooked. Using a spatula, carefully remove stuffed tofu from steamer and place on kitchen paper to drain. Repeat steaming with the other plate of stuffed tofu.

Heat half of the vegetable oil in a large non-stick frying pan or wok until the surface seems to shimmer slightly. Lightly dust half of the tofu triangles in cornflour, shaking off any excess. Carefully slide tofu into the hot oil and fry for 2 minutes each side or until golden and crisp. Remove and drain on kitchen paper, then carefully pour off the used oil. Heat remaining oil in pan or wok, then flour and fry the remaining tofu triangles.

Arrange stuffed tofu on a serving platter, sprinkle with Sichuan pepper and salt and serve with a side dish of chilli–soy dipping sauce.

Serve as a starter for 6–8 (makes 24)

BRAISED SILKEN TOFU WITH CARAMEL SPICED SOY SAUCE AND DEEP-FRIED GARLIC SLICES

Allowing the silken tofu to steep in boiling water for 15 minutes firms it up, so it is less likely to fall apart. Don't be tempted to substitute firm tofu, though, as the texture won't be quite right. This dish is sweet in flavour, and so is best served alongside a more savoury dish to balance the meal. The deep-fried garlic slices add subtle flavour and texture, while the strips of cucumber are refreshingly cool.

1 × 300 g packet silken tofu
½ small cucumber
3 tablespoons Caramel Spiced Soy Sauce (page 294)
pinch Sichuan Pepper and Salt (page 306)

DEEP-FRIED GARLIC SLICES
vegetable oil, for deep-frying
3 garlic cloves, sliced as thinly as possible

Gently remove tofu from packet and invert onto a plate. Cut tofu block into 4 squares. Carefully slide the tofu squares into a bowl and cover with boiling water. Allow to steep for 15 minutes – this will firm up the tofu, making it easier to handle later. Carefully lift the tofu from the water and place on a chopping board, then cut into 1 cm cubes.

Meanwhile, make the deep-fried garlic slices. Heat a 2 cm depth of oil in a small saucepan until the surface seems to shimmer very slightly (130°C). Add garlic and deep-fry for 30 seconds or until lightly golden, stirring constantly – you don't want the garlic to burn and become bitter. Remove with a slotted spoon and drain on paper towel.

Slice cucumber into thin rounds, then cut the rounds into mini-matchsticks. Set aside.

Gently reheat the caramel spiced soy sauce in a wok. Carefully add tofu cubes and gently swirl wok to coat tofu with sauce. Simmer for 2 minutes.

Using a spatula, gently lift out tofu and place in a shallow bowl, then pour over sauce. Garnish with cucumber and deep-fried garlic slices and sprinkle with Sichuan pepper and salt. Serve immediately.

Serve as a side as part of a banquet for 2–4

BRAISED CHINESE MUSHROOMS

No Chinese kitchen is complete without these intensely flavoured mushrooms on hand – having a jar of braised Chinese mushrooms in the fridge is like having 'money in the bank'! They are so versatile and, as you can see, I have included them in many dishes throughout this book, from stir-fries and braises to pickles and stuffings.

12 dried Chinese mushrooms
3 cm × 2 cm knob ginger, finely sliced
1 spring onion, halved
2 garlic cloves, crushed
2 tablespoons shao hsing wine or dry sherry

Soak mushrooms in hot tap water for 1 hour, ensuring that they are completely submerged. Use a small plate to weight them down, if necessary. When softened, remove stems with scissors and discard.

Place mushrooms in a small saucepan and add enough water to cover. Add ginger, spring onion, garlic and wine or sherry, then bring to the boil. Reduce heat and simmer for 20 minutes or until the mushrooms are tender and infused with the flavourings.

Allow to cool in the cooking liquid then store the mushrooms, still in their liquid, in the refrigerator until required – they will keep for a week.

To use, drain the mushrooms well, squeezing out any excess liquid with your hands, then use as directed in recipes.

Makes about 250 g (1 cup) drained mushrooms

Use in

- Chicken and Bean Curd Rolls (page 81)
- Chicken Wings Stuffed with Pork and Prawn (page 82)
- Stir-Fried Lamb with Bamboo Shoots and Chinese Mushrooms (page 107)
- Fish Fillets with Chinese Mushrooms and Lup Cheong Sausage (page 154)
- Stir-Fried Chinese Cabbage with Tofu and Glass Noodles (page 199)
- Stir-fried King Brown and Chinese Mushrooms with Celery (page 200)
- Chinese Mushrooms Stuffed with Prawns, Lup Cheong Sausage and Coriander (page 208)
- Stir-fried Corn, Peas, Chinese Mushrooms and Potato (page 215)

BLANCHED BAMBOO SHOOTS

Fresh bamboo shoots can be difficult to find, but if you do ever come across them I insist that you buy them and have a go at preparing them. There is nothing quite like fresh bamboo, with its straw-like, grassy flavour, wonderful crunch and firm texture. You will *never* eat tinned bamboo shoots again! Compared to fresh, tinned bamboo has a muddy flavour. Now, if I cannot find fresh, I just go without.

1 kg fresh bamboo shoots

3 teaspoons salt flakes

Bring a large saucepan of water to the boil and add 1 teaspoon salt.

Halve bamboo lengthways and remove fibrous husk. You will be left with the tender inner core. Trim the base and ridges from the bamboo, then thinly slice bamboo lengthways.

Add bamboo to boiling water and cook for 5 minutes, then drain and rinse well.

Repeat this blanching process two more times, using fresh boiling salted water each time, and draining and rinsing in between.

Blanching the bamboo three times is an important step, so don't skip it – it removes the bitterness and destroys the hydrocyanic acid bamboo contains.

Makes about 500 g

Use in
- Stir-Fried Lamb with Bamboo Shoots and Chinese Mushrooms (page 107)
- Pickled Bamboo Shoots (page 241)

SALADS AND PICKLES

SALAD OF GLASS NOODLES WITH SHREDDED EGG

I really like glass noodles because of their lightness, which is what makes this such a wonderful summer dish. I include a very generous amount of fresh herbs for extra flavour and aroma; the shredded egg adds substance; and the pickled carrot, along with its pickling liquid, contributes depth of flavour. Feel free to improvise with this salad, using roasted pork slices, fine julienne strips of carrot, finely sliced celery, bean sprouts, prawns or grilled chicken fillets.

100 g glass (bean thread) noodles
3 free-range eggs
1 small cucumber, cut into fine julienne strips
3 red shallots, halved and finely sliced
½ bunch mint, leaves picked
½ bunch coriander, leaves picked
½ bunch dill, leaves picked
½ bunch Vietnamese mint, leaves picked
100 g (heaped ½ cup) drained Pickled Cabbage (page 254), finely shredded
60 g (½ cup) drained Pickled Carrot (page 253)
80 ml (⅓ cup) pickling liquid (from Pickled Carrot)
2½ tablespoons fish sauce

DEEP-FRIED GARLIC SLICES
vegetable oil, for deep-frying
3 garlic cloves, sliced as thinly as possible

Soak noodles in hot tap water for 15 minutes. Drain and refresh under cold running water. Thoroughly drain the noodles again, then place in a large bowl.

Meanwhile, make the deep-fried garlic slices. Heat 2 cm of oil in a small saucepan until the surface seems to shimmer very slightly (130°C). Add garlic and deep-fry for 30 seconds or until lightly golden, stirring constantly – you don't want the garlic to burn and become bitter. Remove with a slotted spoon and drain on paper towel. Reserve 3 tablespoons of the garlic-infused oil and discard the rest.

Line a large plate with kitchen paper. Crack the eggs into a bowl and lightly beat. Heat 1 tablespoon of the reserved garlic oil in a non-stick frying pan over medium–high heat until the surface seems to shimmer slightly. Pour in one-third of the beaten egg and tilt pan to spread egg evenly over base and make an 'egg crepe'. Leave to cook for 1 minute, without disturbing it – the egg will bubble up and become lightly golden underneath. Carefully slide egg crepe onto kitchen paper to drain. Wipe out pan and repeat the process, making 3 egg crepes in total.

When crepes have cooled slightly, roll each one up individually and cut into 3 mm thick shreds.

Just before serving, add most of the shredded egg to the noodles. Add remaining ingredients except garlic chips and, using your hands, toss to combine. Arrange noodle salad on a serving platter and top with deep-fried garlic slices and remaining shredded egg. Serve immediately.

Serve as a main meal for 2 or as part of a banquet for 4

SALAD OF CHINESE CABBAGE, BOK CHOY AND FENNEL WITH TOMATO DRESSING

Chinese cabbage and bok choy are as delicious finely sliced and served raw in salads as they are cooked. Be sure to toss this salad with the dressing just before serving so it doesn't become soggy.

270 g Chinese cabbage (about ¼ medium one), finely shredded
2 spring onions, cut into fine julienne strips
1 bok choy, trimmed and finely sliced
1 small bulb fennel, trimmed and finely sliced
1 bunch mint, leaves picked
½ lemon – optional
pinch Sichuan Pepper and Salt (page 306)

TOMATO DRESSING
2 tablespoons light soy sauce
1 tablespoon brown sugar
juice of 1 lemon
80 ml (⅓ cup) grapeseed oil
3 ripe tomatoes, finely chopped

Combine cabbage, spring onion, bok choy, fennel and mint in a large bowl and mix well.

To make the tomato dressing, combine soy sauce, sugar and lemon juice in a bowl and whisk to dissolve sugar. While whisking, slowly drizzle in the oil, continuing until all of it is incorporated. Add tomato and stir to combine.

Add dressing to salad and toss well using your hands. Transfer to a platter, leaving any excess dressing in bowl, then squeeze the lemon half over the salad, if using, and garnish with Sichuan pepper and salt. Serve immediately.

Serve as part of a banquet for 4–6

SALAD OF FIVE-SPICE TOFU WITH CORIANDER, BEAN SPROUTS AND CHILLI

Five-spice tofu is a great ingredient for vegetarians, and preparing it couldn't be easier: simply slice finely, then toss through salads or add to a stir-fry. With its combination of five-spice tofu, coriander and sesame, this salad is full of fresh flavours.

- 1 × 220 g packet five-spice pressed tofu, finely sliced
- 90 g (1 cup) bean sprouts
- 1 bunch coriander (roots, leaves and stems), washed and roughly chopped
- 1 small cucumber, cut into fine julienne strips

DRESSING

- 2 garlic cloves, finely diced
- 2 tablespoons light soy sauce
- 1¼ tablespoons malt vinegar
- 1 tablespoon white sugar
- 1 teaspoon sesame oil
- 1 teaspoon chilli oil (store-bought – or from Chilli Sauce on page 297)

Combine all of the dressing ingredients in a large bowl and whisk well until the sugar is dissolved.

Add all of the salad ingredients to the dressing and toss well using your hands. Transfer to a platter and serve immediately.

Serves as a starter for 2–4 or as part of a banquet for 4

SALAD OF PRAWNS, PICKLED CAULIFLOWER, PICKLED RED ONION AND BLACK CLOUD EAR FUNGUS

Perhaps the prettiest dish of all – the soft pink liquid of the pickled red onion looks so beautiful against the dark brown cloud-ear fungus and coral-coloured prawns. This is a really simple dish that can be easily assembled just before serving: the pickles will have been made several days or a week beforehand, so all you need to do is sear the prawns and toss together.

140 g (1 cup) drained Pickled Cauliflower (page 242)
130 g (½ cup) drained Pickled Red Onion (page 245), plus 3 tablespoons pickling liquid
50 g fresh black cloud ear fungus (½ packet), cores removed, roughly torn
2½ teaspoons fish sauce
1 tablespoon grapeseed oil
1 tablespoon vegetable oil
12 uncooked medium-sized prawns (350 g), peeled and deveined but with tails intact (180 g peeled)
pinch Spicy Salt (page 305)

Place pickled cauliflower, pickled red onion with its pickling liquid, black cloud ear fungus, fish sauce and grapeseed oil in a large bowl and toss to combine. Set aside.

Heat vegetable oil in a hot wok until the surface seems to shimmer slightly. Carefully place prawns in wok and cook for 30 seconds each side or until cooked through. Remove from the wok and drain on kitchen paper.

Add half of prawns to salad and toss to combine. Transfer to a serving platter and arrange remaining prawns on top. Sprinkle over spicy salt and serve immediately.

Serve as part of a banquet for 4–6

SALAD OF JELLYFISH WITH VINEGAR AND SESAME DRESSING

We Chinese are obsessed with texture and there is no ingredient more textural than jellyfish – I always describe it as being like tender rubber bands! Although it has enormous textural appeal, jellyfish really doesn't really have any flavour, so traditionally it is combined with a pungent dressing of soy sauce, vinegar and sesame oil, which really brings it alive.

1 × 375 g packet salted jellyfish
1 small cucumber, cut into fine julienne strips
2 spring onions, cut into fine julienne strips
90 g (1 cup) bean sprouts
1 tablespoon roasted sesame seeds
pinch Sichuan Pepper and Salt (page 306)

VINEGAR AND SESAME DRESSING
2 tablespoons light soy sauce
2 teaspoons sesame oil
1½ tablespoons malt vinegar
1½ teaspoons white sugar
5 cm × 1 cm knob (15 g) ginger, finely diced

Rinse jellyfish under cold running water for 10 minutes, then drain and soak in fresh water for 1 hour. This removes the saltiness from the jellyfish and rehydrates it.

To make the vinegar and sesame dressing, combine all of the ingredients together in a bowl, stirring to dissolve the sugar.

Drain jellyfish thoroughly and place in a large bowl. Add remaining salad ingredients and dressing and toss well using your hands. Transfer to a plate to serve.

Serve as a starter for 2–4

SALAD OF CARAMELISED DUCK AND LYCHEES

One of the great food combinations: duck and lychees. When lychees are in season I cannot get enough of them. They are such ambrosial, juicy, beautiful-looking fruits, and they also happen to work perfectly with Asian flavours. If you cannot find fresh lychees, use tinned. This recipe also offers a very simple way of cooking duck, which I know can be rather intimidating. The results are superb and the Red Braise Master Stock can be drained and re-used over and over again.

3.5 litres Red Braise Master Stock (page 39)
2 × 180 g–200 g free-range duck breasts, at room temperature
2 tablespoons brown sugar
juice of 1 lime
10 lychees, peeled and seeds removed
3–4 small iceberg lettuce leaves
½ red shallot, finely sliced

Make the red braise master stock in a large saucepan that will hold the duck breasts snugly.

When master stock is ready, return it to the boil. Lower duck breasts into stock, ensuring they are fully submerged – you may need to weight them down with a plate – and poach duck breasts for 5 minutes. There should be no more than an occasional ripple breaking the surface; adjust the temperature, if necessary. Do not put a lid on the pan at any stage.

Immediately remove pan from the heat and allow duck to steep in the stock for 2½–3 hours, or until stock is at room temperature, to complete the cooking process.

Remove duck breasts and cut into 8 mm thick slices on the diagonal.

Strain master stock and reserve 250 ml (1 cup). (Don't forget you can freeze the remainder of the stock to use again.)

Place sugar and reserved master stock in a frying pan and bring to the boil, stirring to dissolve sugar. Cook for 6–7 minutes or until caramelised and reduced – the sauce will bubble up and become sticky. Remove from heat and stir through lime juice and lychees.

Arrange lettuce cups on a platter and arrange duck slices on top. Spoon caramelised sauce and lychees over duck and scatter over shallot slices to serve.

Serve as part of a banquet for 4

SALAD OF RED-BRAISED POUSSIN, BLACK CLOUD EAR FUNGUS AND CELERY

I love small birds, and the poussins available nowadays are incredibly juicy, meaty and affordable. This beautiful salad could also be made with leftover chicken. The pickled celery adds depth of flavour, but any other type of pickle could be used here instead – try Pickled Mixed Mushrooms (page 258) or Pickled Cucumber (page 250).

3.5 litres Red Braise Master Stock (page 39)
1 × 500 g free-range poussin (spatchcock), at room temperature
50 g fresh black cloud ear fungus (½ packet), cores removed, roughly torn
1 bunch coriander, leaves picked
1 teaspoon light soy sauce
½ teaspoon sesame oil
½ teaspoon Chilli Salt (page 305)

QUICK PICKLED CELERY
2 sticks celery, trimmed and cut into 5 cm long matchsticks
1 teaspoon salt flakes
1 teaspoon white sugar
juice of 1 lemon

Make the red braise master stock in a large saucepan that will hold the poussin comfortably.

Rinse poussin under cold water. Trim away excess fat from inside and outside the cavity. Cut off the neck, parson's nose and winglets and discard. Pat dry with kitchen paper.

When master stock is ready, return it to the boil. Lower poussin, breast-side down, into stock, ensuring it is fully submerged – you may need to weight it down with a plate – and poach poussin for exactly 6 minutes. There should be no more than an occasional ripple breaking the surface; adjust the temperature, if necessary. Do not put a lid on the pan at any stage.

Immediately remove pan from the heat and allow poussin to steep in the stock for 1½ hours at room temperature to complete the cooking process.

Meanwhile, make the quick pickled celery. Place celery, salt and sugar in a bowl and combine well with your hands. Refrigerate for 30 minutes.

Using tongs, gently remove poussin from the stock and place on a tray or large plate to drain. Place the poussin, breast-side up, on a chopping board and halve lengthways. Cut the thighs where they meet the body and remove the legs. Cut the wings where they meet the body and remove. Gently shred flesh and skin (it's the best bit!) into large chunks, place in a bowl and set aside. (You should get about 230 g meat.) Discard the bones.

Reserve 3 tablespoons of the master stock. Fish out 3 pieces of the red-braised ginger from the stock and slice thinly. (Don't forget you can strain and freeze the remainder of the stock to use again.)

Drain pickled celery well, squeezing with your hands to remove any excess liquid, then toss with lemon juice. Add poussin meat, reserved master stock, red-braised ginger slices, black cloud ear fungus, coriander, soy sauce and sesame oil and mix well. Arrange on a platter and sprinkle over chilli salt to serve.

Serve as a starter for 4

PICKLED BAMBOO SHOOTS (LEFT)

Fresh bamboo shoots are so versatile. As they're not always easy to find, when I do come across them, I like to pickle them, so they're ready to serve in a salad or as a side dish – I find they go particularly well alongside chicken and prawn dishes.

250 g Blanched Bamboo Shoots (page 223)
1 tablespoon salt flakes

PICKLING LIQUID
1 litre (4 cups) white vinegar
295 g (1⅓ cups) white sugar

To make the pickling liquid, combine vinegar and sugar in a heavy-based saucepan and stir over high heat until sugar dissolves. Bring to the boil, then reduce to a simmer and cook, uncovered and without stirring, for about 30 minutes or until reduced by one-third and slightly syrupy. Set aside to cool, then refrigerate overnight.

Place bamboo in a large bowl, sprinkle with salt and mix well to combine. Cover and refrigerate overnight.

The next day, drain liquid from bamboo and squeeze with your hands to remove any excess liquid. Place bamboo in a 1 litre (4 cup) capacity airtight jar or container and pour pickling liquid over to cover. Refrigerate for 2 days to allow flavours to develop before using. The pickled bamboo shoots will keep for up to 2 weeks in the fridge.

Makes 250 g (about 1½ cups) drained

PICKLED WHITE RADISH (RIGHT)

I like to serve this pickle with seafood – it's wonderful with sashimi, or with cooked prawns, crab or lobster – but it can also be simply served as a side dish to a shared meal.

300 g white radish (daikon)
1 tablespoon salt flakes
5 cm × 2 cm knob (20 g) ginger, thickly sliced
¼ teaspoon Sichuan peppercorns

PICKLING LIQUID
500 ml (2 cups) white vinegar
145 g (⅔ cup) white sugar

To make the pickling liquid, combine vinegar and sugar in a heavy-based saucepan and stir over high heat until sugar dissolves. Bring to the boil, then reduce to a simmer and cook, uncovered and without stirring, for about 20 minutes or until reduced by one-third and slightly syrupy. Set aside to cool, then refrigerate overnight.

Meanwhile, peel and halve radish lengthways then cut each half into 5 mm thick half-moons. Place radish in a large bowl, sprinkle with salt and mix well to combine. Cover and refrigerate overnight.

The next day, drain liquid from radish and squeeze with your hands to remove any excess liquid. Place radish in a 1 litre (4 cup) capacity airtight jar or container, pour pickling liquid over to cover and add ginger and peppercorns. Refrigerate for 1 day to allow flavours to develop before using. The pickled radish will keep for up to 2 weeks in the fridge.

Makes 260 g (1½ cups) drained

PICKLED CAULIFLOWER (LEFT)

Cauliflower is fantastic pickled, as it retains its crunch. This version can be served with either Chinese or Western-style meals – it makes a great appetiser.

½ small cauliflower (about 500 g), core removed, cut into florets
1 tablespoon salt flakes
3 dried small red chillies

PICKLING LIQUID
1 litre (4 cups) white vinegar
295 g (1⅓ cups) white sugar

To make the pickling liquid, combine vinegar and sugar in a heavy-based saucepan and stir over high heat until sugar dissolves. Bring to the boil, then reduce to a simmer and cook, uncovered and without stirring, for about 30 minutes or until reduced by one-third and slightly syrupy. Set aside to cool, then refrigerate overnight.

Meanwhile, place cauliflower in a large bowl, sprinkle with salt and mix well to combine. Cover and refrigerate overnight.

The next day, drain liquid from cauliflower. Place cauliflower in a 1 litre (4 cup) capacity airtight jar or container, pour pickling liquid over to cover and add chillies. Refrigerate for 1 day to allow flavours to develop before using. The pickled cauliflower will keep for up to 2 weeks in the fridge.

Makes 275 g (2 cups) drained

Use in • Salad of Prawns, Pickled Cauliflower, Pickled Red Onion and Black Cloud Ear Fungus (page 233)

PICKLED CHINESE CABBAGE (RIGHT)

This is perfect as a small, tasty dish to nibble on with drinks, perhaps with some roasted peanuts too. It can also be tossed into stir-fried meat or poultry dishes, or finely sliced and added to salads.

½ Chinese cabbage (about 600 g)
1 tablespoon salt flakes
2 garlic cloves, crushed
5 cm × 2 cm knob (20 g) ginger, thickly sliced

PICKLING LIQUID
1 litre (4 cups) white vinegar
295 g (1⅓ cups) white sugar

To make the pickling liquid, combine vinegar and sugar in a heavy-based saucepan and stir over high heat until sugar dissolves. Bring to the boil, then reduce to a simmer and cook, uncovered and without stirring, for about 30 minutes or until reduced by one-third and slightly syrupy. Set aside to cool, then refrigerate overnight.

Meanwhile, discard the outer darker green leaves of the cabbage and cut out the core. Separate leaves and slice each leaf crossways into 2 cm thick slices. Place in a large bowl, sprinkle with salt and mix well to combine. Cover and refrigerate overnight.

The next day, drain liquid from cabbage and squeeze with your hands to remove any excess liquid. Place cabbage in a 1 litre (4 cup) capacity airtight jar or container, pour pickling liquid over to cover and add garlic and ginger. Refrigerate for 2–3 days to allow flavours to develop before using. The pickled cabbage will keep for up to 2 weeks in the fridge.

Makes 250 g (about 2 cups) drained

PICKLED RED ONION (LEFT)

I serve these pickles with seafood in this book, but they go equally well with meat and poultry dishes.

3 small red onions (about 350 g)
1 tablespoon salt flakes
5 cm × 2 cm knob (20 g) ginger, thickly sliced
¼ teaspoon Sichuan peppercorns

PICKLING LIQUID
500 ml (2 cups) white vinegar
145 g (⅔ cup) white sugar

To make the pickling liquid, combine vinegar and sugar in a heavy-based saucepan and stir over high heat until sugar dissolves. Bring to the boil, then reduce to a simmer and cook, uncovered and without stirring, for about 20 minutes or until reduced by one-third and slightly syrupy. Set aside to cool, then refrigerate overnight.

Meanwhile, cut onions in half, then cut lengthways into 3 mm thick slices. Place in a bowl, sprinkle with salt and mix well to combine. Cover and refrigerate overnight.

The next day, drain liquid from onion, squeezing it well with your hands. Place onion in a 1 litre (4 cup) capacity airtight jar or container, pour pickling liquid over to cover and add ginger and peppercorns. Refrigerate for 1 day to allow flavours to develop before using. The pickled onion will keep for up to 2 weeks in the fridge.

Makes 260 g (2 cups) drained

Use in
- Fried Oysters with Chilli Salt and Pickled Red Onion (page 137)
- Salad of Prawns, Pickled Cauliflower, Pickled Red Onion and Black Cloud Ear Fungus (page 233)

PICKLED FENNEL (RIGHT)

I love to pickle fennel when it's in season – the young bulbs are just so flavoursome and tender. Serve alone or with meats, especially pork.

600 g baby fennel
1 tablespoon salt flakes
2 garlic cloves, crushed
1 star anise
2 dried small red chillies

PICKLING LIQUID
1 litre (4 cups) white vinegar
295 g (1⅓ cups) white sugar

To make the pickling liquid, combine vinegar and sugar in a heavy-based saucepan and stir over high heat until sugar dissolves. Bring to the boil, then reduce to a simmer and cook, uncovered and without stirring, for about 30 minutes or until reduced by one-third and slightly syrupy. Set aside to cool, then refrigerate overnight.

Meanwhile, trim each fennel bulb, stand on its base and halve lengthways. Cut out the core and discard any fibrous outer segments. Slice each half crossways into 5 mm thick slices. Place fennel in a large bowl, sprinkle with salt and mix well to combine. Cover bowl and refrigerate overnight.

The next day, drain liquid from fennel, squeezing it well with your hands. Place fennel in a 1 litre (4 cup) capacity airtight jar or container, pour pickling liquid over to cover and add garlic, star anise and chillies. Refrigerate for 2 days to allow flavours to develop before using. The pickled fennel will keep for up to 2 weeks in the fridge.

Makes 340 g (about 2½ cups) drained

PICKLED RED RADISH (LEFT)

Serve this alone or mix it with other pickles, such as carrot, cauliflower and cucumber, to create a stunning appetiser or side dish. The little half-moon shapes shrivel up slightly in the pickling solution, but still retain their appealing colour and crunch.

500 g red radishes, washed and trimmed
1 tablespoon salt flakes
3 garlic cloves, crushed

PICKLING LIQUID
1 litre (4 cups) white vinegar
295 g (1⅓ cups) white sugar

To make the pickling liquid, combine vinegar and sugar in a heavy-based saucepan and stir over high heat until sugar dissolves. Bring to the boil, then reduce to a simmer and cook, uncovered and without stirring, for about 30 minutes or until reduced by one-third and slightly syrupy. Set aside to cool, then refrigerate overnight.

Meanwhile, slice each radish into quarters, or eighths if large. Place radish in a large bowl, sprinkle with salt and mix well to combine. Cover and refrigerate overnight.

The next day, drain off liquid from radish and squeeze with your hands to remove any excess liquid. Place radish in a 1 litre (4 cup) capacity airtight jar or container, pour pickling liquid over to cover and add garlic. Refrigerate for 3 days to allow flavours to develop before using. The pickled radish will keep for up to 2 weeks in the fridge.

Makes 360 g (2½ cups) drained

PICKLED BEETROOT (RIGHT)

Pickling beetroot really brings out its delicious, earthy flavour, not to mention its stunning, deep, dark burgundy colour. This robust pickle goes well with rich meats and pork.

3 beetroot (about 400 g in total)
1 tablespoon salt flakes
5 cm × 2 cm knob (20 g) ginger, thickly sliced
1 star anise

PICKLING LIQUID
500 ml (2 cups) white vinegar
145 g (⅔ cup) white sugar

To make the pickling liquid, combine vinegar and sugar in a heavy-based saucepan and stir over high heat until sugar dissolves. Bring to the boil, then reduce to a simmer and cook, uncovered and without stirring, for about 20 minutes or until reduced by one-third and slightly syrupy. Set aside to cool, then refrigerate overnight.

Meanwhile, peel and cut the beetroot into thin wedges. Place in a bowl, sprinkle with salt and mix well to combine. Cover and refrigerate overnight.

The next day, drain liquid from beetroot and place in a 1 litre (4 cup) capacity airtight jar or container. Pour pickling liquid over to cover and add ginger and star anise. Refrigerate for 1 week to allow flavours to develop before using. The pickled beetroot will keep for up to 2 weeks in the fridge.

Makes 250 g (2 cups) drained

Use in • White-Cooked Pork Belly with Pickles and Blistered Chillies (page 108)

PICKLED EGGPLANT (LEFT)

Eggplant becomes quite intense and rich when pickled, so only serve small quantities. This pickle goes well with rich meat dishes – lamb, duck, quail, pigeon and roasted or deep-fried chicken – as well as oily fish.

1 small eggplant (aubergine) – about 300 g
1 tablespoon salt flakes
2 garlic cloves, crushed
2 dried small red chillies

PICKLING LIQUID
1 litre (4 cups) white vinegar
295 g (1⅓ cups) white sugar

To make the pickling liquid, combine vinegar and sugar in a heavy-based saucepan and stir over high heat until sugar dissolves. Bring to the boil, then reduce to a simmer and cook, uncovered and without stirring, for about 30 minutes or until reduced by one-third and slightly syrupy. Set aside to cool, then refrigerate overnight.

Meanwhile, trim the eggplant and halve lengthways, then slice crossways into 5 mm thick half-moons. Place in a bowl, sprinkle with salt and mix well to combine. Cover and refrigerate overnight.

The next day, drain liquid from eggplant and squeeze with your hands to remove any excess liquid. Place eggplant in a 1 litre (4 cup) capacity airtight jar or container, pour pickling liquid over to cover and add garlic and chillies. Refrigerate for 1 day to allow flavours to develop before using. The pickled eggplant will keep for up to 2 weeks in the fridge.

Makes 290 g (about 2 cups) drained

PICKLED GINGER (RIGHT)

It's always handy to have a jar of pickled ginger in the fridge. You can serve it as a side dish to sashimi, or incorporate it into dishes such as stir-fried calamari, or stir-fried chicken to enhance the overall flavour. You can also cut it into fine julienne strips and use it to add a punchy, refreshing note to salads. Try to find tender young ginger for pickling, rather than older, more fibrous pieces.

350 g young ginger
1 tablespoon salt flakes

PICKLING LIQUID
500 ml (2 cups) white vinegar
145 g (⅔ cup) white sugar

To make the pickling liquid, combine vinegar and sugar in a heavy-based saucepan and stir over high heat until sugar dissolves. Bring to the boil, then reduce to a simmer and cook, uncovered and without stirring, for about 20 minutes or until reduced by one-third and slightly syrupy. Set aside to cool, then refrigerate overnight.

Meanwhile, peel and cut the ginger into 1 mm thick slices. Place in a bowl, sprinkle with salt and mix well to combine. Cover and refrigerate overnight.

The next day, drain liquid from ginger and squeeze with your hands to remove any excess liquid. Place ginger in a 1 litre (4 cup) capacity airtight jar or container and pour pickling liquid over to cover. Refrigerate for at least 1 week to allow flavours to develop before using. You can use the pickled ginger earlier, but it will still be quite peppery. Once it is ready, it will keep for 3–4 weeks in the fridge.

Makes 200 g (about 1 cup) drained

PICKLED CUCUMBER (LEFT)

I just love pickled cucumber – mostly for its texture, which is sort of crunchy yet wilted and soft at the same time. Serve it alone or with meat and poultry dishes.

3 small cucumbers (about 400 g), trimmed
1 tablespoon salt flakes
2 garlic cloves, crushed
5 cm × 2 cm knob (20 g) ginger, thickly sliced
2 dried small red chillies
¼ teaspoon Sichuan peppercorns

PICKLING LIQUID
500 ml (2 cups) white vinegar
145 g (⅔ cup) white sugar

To make the pickling liquid, combine vinegar and sugar in a heavy-based saucepan and stir over high heat until sugar dissolves. Bring to the boil, then reduce to a simmer and cook, uncovered and without stirring, for about 20 minutes or until reduced by one-third and slightly syrupy. Set aside to cool, then refrigerate overnight.

Meanwhile, halve cucumbers lengthways and scoop out the seeds using a teaspoon. Slice each piece into half-moons. Place cucumbers in a large bowl, sprinkle with salt and mix well to combine. Cover and refrigerate overnight.

The next day, drain liquid from cucumber, squeezing it well with your hand. Place cucumber in a 1 litre (4 cup) capacity airtight jar or container, pour pickling liquid over to cover and add garlic, ginger, chillies and peppercorns. Refrigerate for 1 day to allow flavours to develop before using. The pickled cucumber will keep for up to 2 weeks in the fridge.

Makes 250 g (2 cups) drained

Use in
- Quail with Chilli–Soy Dipping Sauce and Pickled Cucumber (page 78)
- White-Cooked Pork Belly with Pickles and Blistered Chillies (page 108)
- Crispy-Skin Eggs, Caramelised Chicken and Pickles (page 174)

PICKLED ZUCCHINI (RIGHT)

Because this pickle is quite pungent, I suggest serving it with meat dishes, though it's also good finely sliced and added to Sung Choi Bao of Vegetables (page 192).

3 small zucchini (courgettes) – about 400 g – trimmed
1 tablespoon salt flakes
2 garlic cloves, smashed

PICKLING LIQUID
500 ml (2 cups) white vinegar
145 g (⅔ cup) white sugar

To make the pickling liquid, combine vinegar and sugar in a heavy-based saucepan and stir over high heat until sugar dissolves. Bring to the boil, then reduce to a simmer and cook, uncovered and without stirring, for about 20 minutes or until reduced by one-third and slightly syrupy. Set aside to cool, then refrigerate overnight.

Meanwhile, halve zucchini lengthways, then cut in half crossways and cut each quarter into batons. Place zucchini in a large bowl, sprinkle with salt and mix well to combine. Cover and refrigerate overnight.

The next day, drain liquid from zucchini, squeezing it well with your hands. Place zucchini in a 1 litre (4 cup) capacity airtight jar or container, pour pickling liquid over to cover and add garlic. Refrigerate for 1 day to allow flavours to develop before using. The pickled zucchini will keep for up to 2 weeks in the fridge.

Makes 310 g (about 2 cups) drained

PICKLED BRAISED CHINESE MUSHROOMS (LEFT)

I really like the intense flavour and meaty yet tender texture of these dried mushrooms. They enhance any dish they are served with – just remember that you only need a small amount as they are rather rich.

2 tablespoons peanut oil
5 cm × 4 cm knob (30 g) ginger, cut into fine julienne strips
12 Braised Chinese Mushrooms (page 220), stems discarded and caps finely sliced
2 teaspoons brown sugar
2 tablespoons light soy sauce
1 tablespoon malt vinegar

Heat oil in a hot wok until the surface seems to shimmer slightly. Add ginger and mushrooms and stir-fry for 2 minutes for flavours to combine. Reduce heat to medium, add sugar and stir-fry for 30 seconds to caramelise. Add soy sauce and vinegar and stir-fry for 1 minute.

Serve hot or allow to cool. Store in an airtight container in the refrigerator for up to 5 days.

Makes 250 g (1 cup)

Use in • Beef Fillet with Roasted Rice and Pickled Chinese Mushrooms (page 92)

PICKLED CARROT (RIGHT)

I am always using pickled carrots in my dishes. This simple pickling technique transforms them so dramatically that I find adding pickled carrot to a salad of vegetables or noodles, for example, turns an ordinary dish into an extraordinary one.

3 carrots (about 300 g in total)
1 tablespoon salt flakes
5 cm × 2 cm knob (20 g) ginger, thickly sliced
1 star anise
¼ teaspoon Sichuan peppercorns

PICKLING LIQUID
1 litre (4 cups) white vinegar
295 g (1⅓ cups) white sugar

To make the pickling liquid, combine vinegar and sugar in a heavy-based saucepan and stir over high heat until sugar dissolves. Bring to the boil, then reduce to a simmer and cook, uncovered and without stirring, for about 30 minutes or until reduced by one-third and slightly syrupy. Set aside to cool, then refrigerate overnight.

Meanwhile, peel each carrot and cut in half crossways. Cut each piece into 2 mm thick slices, then into matchsticks. Place in a bowl, sprinkle with salt and mix well to combine. Cover and refrigerate overnight.

The next day, drain liquid from carrot, squeezing it well with your hands. Place carrot in a 1 litre (4 cup) capacity airtight jar or container, pour pickling liquid over to cover and add ginger, star anise and peppercorns. Refrigerate for 1 day to allow flavours to develop before using. The pickled carrot will keep for up to 2 weeks in the fridge.

Makes 300 g (about 2½ cups) drained

Use in • Thin Egg Noodle Salad with Roasted Pork, Pickled Carrot and Sesame Seeds (page 274)
• Salad of Glass Noodles with Shredded Egg (page 226)

PICKLED RED SHALLOTS (LEFT)

Serve these in the same way you would serve pickled onions: with meat or grilled seafood, on a sandwich or hamburger, or as a side dish. The pickling liquid takes on the softest pink colour from the shallots, and is beautiful added to salad dressings.

300 g red shallots (about 3 or 4)
1 tablespoon salt flakes
5 cm × 2 cm knob (20 g) ginger, thickly sliced
¼ teaspoon Sichuan peppercorns

PICKLING LIQUID
500 ml (2 cups) white vinegar
145 g (⅔ cup) white sugar

To make the pickling liquid, combine vinegar and sugar in a heavy-based saucepan and stir over high heat until sugar dissolves. Bring to the boil, then reduce to a simmer and cook, uncovered and without stirring, for about 20 minutes or until reduced by one-third and slightly syrupy. Set aside to cool, then refrigerate overnight.

Meanwhile, trim and cut the shallots into 3 mm thick rings. Separate rings, place in a bowl, sprinkle with salt and mix well to combine. Cover and refrigerate overnight.

The next day, drain liquid from shallots and squeeze with your hands to remove any excess liquid. Place shallots in a 1 litre (4 cup) capacity airtight jar or container, pour pickling liquid over to cover and add ginger and peppercorns. Refrigerate for at least 3 days to allow flavours to develop before using. The pickled shallots will keep for up to 2 weeks in the fridge.

Makes 285 g (about 2 cups) drained

PICKLED CABBAGE (RIGHT)

This is especially good with pork dishes, but also works well as an appetiser by itself, or with other vegetable dishes. The addition of star anise and chilli adds extra complexity.

⅓ white or green cabbage (about 300 g)
1 tablespoon salt flakes
2 dried small red chillies
1 star anise
¼ teaspoon Sichuan peppercorns

PICKLING LIQUID
1 litre (4 cups) white vinegar
295 g (1⅓ cups) white sugar

To make the pickling liquid, combine vinegar and sugar in a heavy-based saucepan and stir over high heat until sugar dissolves. Bring to the boil, then reduce to a simmer and cook, uncovered and without stirring, for about 30 minutes or until reduced by one-third and slightly syrupy. Set aside to cool, then refrigerate overnight.

Meanwhile, remove core from cabbage and cut into pieces about 5 cm × 2 cm. Roughly pull pieces apart to separate leaves. Place cabbage in a large bowl, sprinkle with salt and mix well to combine. Cover and refrigerate overnight.

The next day, drain liquid from cabbage and squeeze with your hands to remove any excess liquid. Place cabbage in a 1 litre (4 cup) capacity airtight jar or container, pour pickling liquid over to cover and add chillies, star anise and peppercorns. Refrigerate for 1 day to allow flavours to develop before using. The pickled cabbage will keep for up to 2 weeks in the fridge.

Makes 250 g (about 1 cup) drained

Use in • Salad of Glass Noodles with Shredded Egg (page 226)

PICKLED CELERY (LEFT)

Pickled celery works particularly well with chicken or egg dishes.

3 large sticks celery
1 tablespoon salt flakes
3 dried small red chillies

PICKLING LIQUID
500 ml (2 cups) white vinegar
145 g (⅔ cup) white sugar

To make the pickling liquid, combine vinegar and sugar in a heavy-based saucepan and stir over high heat until sugar dissolves. Bring to the boil, then reduce to a simmer and cook, uncovered and without stirring, for about 20 minutes or until reduced by one-third and slightly syrupy. Set aside to cool, then refrigerate overnight.

Meanwhile, trim the tops and bottoms off the celery, then cut each stick into 5 mm thick slices on the diagonal. Place celery in a large bowl, sprinkle with salt and mix well to combine. Cover and refrigerate overnight.

The next day, drain liquid from celery and squeeze with your hands to remove any excess liquid. Place celery in a 1 litre (4 cup) capacity airtight jar or container, pour pickling liquid over to cover and add chillies. Refrigerate for at least 2 days to allow flavours to develop before using. The flavour and texture will improve the longer you leave the celery to pickle – it will keep for up to 2 weeks in the fridge.

Makes 250 g (2 cups) drained

PICKLED CHILLIES (RIGHT)

Although large chillies tend to be sweetish rather than spicy, their flavour intensifies when they are pickled. I add bird's eye chillies to give these pickles a real kick of heat, but feel free to use any type of chilli you like.

6 large red chillies
6 large green chillies
4 red bird's eye chillies
2 teaspoons salt flakes
2 garlic cloves, crushed

PICKLING LIQUID
500 ml (2 cups) white vinegar
145 g (⅔ cup) white sugar

To make the pickling liquid, combine vinegar and sugar in a heavy-based saucepan and stir over high heat until sugar dissolves. Bring to the boil, then reduce to a simmer and cook, uncovered and without stirring, for about 20 minutes or until reduced by one-third and slightly syrupy. Set aside to cool, then refrigerate overnight.

Meanwhile, trim stems off chillies, cut in half lengthways and remove seeds with a spoon. Leave bird's eye chillies whole but lightly bruise with the flat blade of a knife. Place chillies in a large bowl, sprinkle with salt and mix well to combine. Cover and refrigerate overnight.

The next day, drain liquid and place chillies in a 1 litre (4 cup) capacity airtight jar or container. Pour pickling liquid over to cover and add garlic. Refrigerate for 1 day to allow flavours to develop before using. The pickled chillies will keep for up to 2 weeks in the fridge.

Makes 180 g (about 1 cup) drained

Use in • Stir-Fried Chicken with Tea-Smoked Oysters and Pickled Chillies (page 69)
• Crispy-Skin Eggs, Caramelised Chicken and Pickles (page 174)

PICKLED MIXED MUSHROOMS

I'd never pickled fresh mushrooms before, so this recipe turned out to be a very pleasant surprise. I use an assortment of fresh Asian mushrooms, which soak up all the flavours of the pickling liquid like sponges, becoming incredibly potent. These go beautifully with braised duck or any other rich meats. I find that this pickle is at its best within a week of being made – beyond that, although still fine to eat, it can become too strong.

300 g mixed mushrooms, such as shiitake, oyster, shimeji and Swiss browns
1 tablespoon salt flakes
2 garlic cloves
2 dried small red chillies

PICKLING LIQUID
500 ml (2 cups) white vinegar
145 g (⅔ cup) white sugar

To make the pickling liquid, combine vinegar and sugar in a heavy-based saucepan and stir over high heat until sugar dissolves. Bring to the boil, then reduce to a simmer and cook, uncovered and without stirring, for about 20 minutes or until reduced by one-third and slightly syrupy. Set aside to cool, then refrigerate overnight.

Meanwhile, trim any woody stems from the mushrooms and cut into even-sized pieces. Place in a bowl, sprinkle with salt and mix well to combine. Cover and refrigerate overnight.

The next day, drain liquid from mushrooms and squeeze with your hands to remove any excess liquid. Place mushrooms in a 1 litre (4 cup) capacity airtight jar or container, pour pickling liquid over to cover and add garlic and chillies. Refrigerate for 1 day to allow flavours to develop before using. The pickled mushrooms will keep for up to 1 week in the fridge.

Makes 250 g (about 1 cup) drained

Use in • Red-Braised Duck Breast with Pickled Mushrooms (page 87)

RICE, NOODLES AND DUMPLINGS

STEAMED RICE

I find that this absorption method always works perfectly. Use any leftover rice for fried rice – day-old steamed rice makes the best fried rice.

265 g (1⅓ cups) uncooked jasmine rice

Place rice in a sieve and rinse under running water until water runs clear. Drain thoroughly.

Combine rice and 500 ml (2 cups) water in a heavy-based saucepan and bring to the boil. Immediately cover with a tight-fitting lid, reduce heat to low and cook for 10 minutes. Do not remove lid during cooking.

Remove from heat and fluff rice with a fork. Replace lid and leave undisturbed for 10 minutes to steam.

Serves 4 – makes 750 g (4 cups) cooked rice

Use in
- Fried Rice with Roasted Pork (page 269)
- Fried Rice with XO Sauce (page 270)

VEGETARIAN STICKY RICE PARCELS

Glutinous rice is much-loved in the Asian kitchen for its wonderfully comforting, sticky texture. It is really simple to cook, but is best steamed, so the rice grains don't become waterlogged. Here the steamed sticky rice is wrapped in bamboo leaves, which add a gorgeous earthy, straw-like aroma and flavour that permeates the rice. The eggs are delicious but optional; if you decide to omit them, just fill each parcel with a little extra rice.

265 g (1⅓ cups) white glutinous rice
1 tablespoon light soy sauce
1 teaspoon malt vinegar
1 teaspoon white sugar
1 teaspoon sesame oil
2 tablespoons peanut oil
5 cm × 4 cm knob (30 g) ginger, cut into fine julienne strips
1 small red onion, halved and finely sliced
4 Braised Chinese Mushrooms (page 220), finely sliced
120 g (¾ cup) salted radish, finely chopped
80 g preserved mustard greens, finely chopped
2 tablespoons shao hsing wine or dry sherry
4 spring onions, finely sliced
6 free-range eggs, at room temperature
about 15 dried bamboo leaves
about 12 short bamboo skewers

Soak glutinous rice in a bowl of cold water for 1 hour, then drain.

Bring a large saucepan or wok of water to the boil. Place rice in a large steamer basket lined with muslin or a clean Chux or J-Cloth. Spread rice out evenly over the base, cover with the lid and position over the pan or wok of boiling water. Steam for 20 minutes or until the rice grains are cooked and no longer chalky.

Combine soy sauce, vinegar, sugar and sesame oil in a bowl.

Heat peanut oil in a hot wok until the surface seems to shimmer slightly. Add ginger, onion, mushrooms, salted radish and mustard greens and stir-fry for 1 minute. Add wine or sherry and let it bubble away and cook out for 30 seconds. Add soy sauce mixture and stir-fry for 1 minute to mix well. Add cooked rice and spring onion and stir-fry for 1 minute to combine thoroughly. Spread the rice mixture out evenly over a large tray or plate to cool.

Meanwhile, place eggs in a small saucepan of boiling water and cook for 7 minutes (or 8 minutes if using eggs straight from the fridge). Remove eggs using a slotted spoon and refresh under cold water. Carefully peel eggs and drain on kitchen paper to remove excess liquid, then halve.

Next soak the bamboo leaves and make the sticky rice parcels (page 266).

Bring a large saucepan or wok of water to the boil. Place parcels in a shallow heatproof bowl that will fit inside a steamer basket. Place bowl inside steamer and cover with the lid. Position over the pan or wok of boiling water and steam for about 10 minutes or until rice filling is warmed through.

Carefully lift out parcels and place on a platter. Remove skewers and unravel the top half of the bamboo leaves to reveal the rice.

Serve as a side dish for 6–8 as part of banquet or as a main for 4 (makes 10–12)

MAKING STICKY RICE PARCELS

❶ Soak bamboo leaves in a bowl of warm water for 1 hour or until malleable. You will need 10–12, but I always soak a few extra as sometimes some of the leaves may tear or break when wrapping the parcels. Leave them soaking in water until ready to make the parcels, then drain well.

❷ Hold a bamboo leaf in one hand with the tip facing up and the underside facing you.

❺ Place half an egg on top, cut-side up, making sure it sits flush with the top of the cone.

❻ Fold the bamboo leaf tightly down and around the cone.

❸ Fold the bottom third of the leaf up and twist the outer edge in on itself to make a small cone. Roll the cone tighter, if necessary, making sure there is no hole at the pointy end.

❹ Spoon enough rice mixture into the cone to fill it nearly to the top, pressing the rice down with your fingers to pack it tightly in the cone.

❼ Keep folding to form a triangular parcel. It's important to roll the parcel as tightly as possible, trying to cover the corners of the parcel completely.

❽ When you get to the end of the leaf, tuck the tip into one of the folds and pierce with a skewer through the centre to secure the leaf.

FRIED RICE WITH ROASTED PORK

This is a basic fried rice recipe, so feel free to add your favourite ingredients. With roasted pork as here, it makes an easy meal-in-one. I sometimes use BBQ pork from Chinatown for a quick meal, or you could use some leftover Roasted Pork Shoulder with Miso and Honey (page 119) for a more dressed-up version.

2 tablespoons light soy sauce
2 teaspoons white sugar
1 teaspoon salt flakes
½ teaspoon sesame oil
4 free-range eggs
2 tablespoons peanut oil, plus 1 teaspoon extra if needed
1 small white onion, finely diced
5 cm × 2 cm knob (20 g) ginger, finely diced
250 g roasted pork, cut into 1 cm batons
2 tablespoons shao hsing wine or dry sherry
750 g (4 cups) Steamed Rice (page 262)
2 spring onions, finely sliced
sliced red chillies in light soy sauce or homemade pickles (pages 241–258), to serve (optional)

Combine soy sauce, sugar, salt and sesame oil in a bowl and set aside.

Crack eggs into a bowl and beat lightly with a fork until just combined.

Heat 2 tablespoons oil in a hot wok until the surface seems to shimmer slightly. Pour in beaten egg and leave to cook on base of wok for 10 seconds, without stirring. Using a spatula, fold egg mixture over onto itself and leave to cook for another 30 seconds. Fold over again and leave for 30 seconds or until almost set. Carefully remove omelette from wok with a spatula and drain on kitchen paper. Set aside.

Add extra oil to wok, if necessary, then add onion, ginger and pork and stir-fry for 1 minute. Pour in wine or sherry and cook for 30 seconds.

Add rice to wok and leave to cook, without stirring, for 2 minutes so a lightly golden crust forms on the underside of the rice.

Add soy sauce mixture, spring onion and reserved omelette and stir-fry for 1 minute so the sauce evenly coats the grains. Use a spatula to break up the omelette into smaller pieces while cooking.

Transfer rice to a serving bowl. Accompany with a side dish of fresh chillies or homemade pickles, if desired.

Serve as a main for 2

FRIED RICE WITH XO SAUCE

It's always handy to have a jar of XO sauce in the fridge, as it is so versatile and can transform ordinary dishes into rather spectacular ones. The spicy, savoury flavour and chewy texture of the XO works perfectly with fried rice, and I also like to add bean sprouts and iceberg at the end for some crunch.

---

3 tablespoons XO Sauce (page 298)
1 tablespoon light soy sauce
1 teaspoon malt vinegar
1 teaspoon salt flakes
½ teaspoon white sugar
½ teaspoon sesame oil
4 free-range eggs
2 tablespoons peanut oil, plus 1 teaspoon extra if needed
1 small red onion, finely diced
5 cm × 2 cm knob (20 g) ginger, finely diced
1 tablespoon shao hsing wine or dry sherry
750 g (4 cups) Steamed Rice (page 262)
2 spring onions, finely sliced
2 small iceberg lettuce leaves, finely shredded
135 g (1½ cups) bean sprouts
pinch Sichuan pepper and salt (page 306)

Combine XO sauce, soy sauce, vinegar, salt, sugar and sesame oil in a bowl.

Crack eggs into a bowl and beat lightly with a fork until just combined.

Heat 2 tablespoons oil in a hot wok until the surface seems to shimmer slightly. Pour in beaten egg and leave to cook on base of wok for 10 seconds, without stirring. Using a spatula, fold egg mixture over onto itself and leave to cook for another 30 seconds. Fold over again and leave for 30 seconds or until almost set. Carefully remove omelette from wok with a spatula and drain on kitchen paper. Set aside.

Add remaining oil to wok, if necessary, then add onion and ginger and stir-fry for 1 minute. Pour in wine or sherry and cook for 30 seconds. Add XO sauce mixture and stir-fry for 1 minute.

Add rice to wok and stir through the sauce to evenly coat the grains. Leave to cook, without stirring, for 2 minutes so a lightly golden crust forms on the underside of the rice.

Add spring onion and reserved omelette and stir-fry for 1 minute. Use a spatula to break up the omelette into smaller pieces while cooking.

Turn off the heat and quickly toss through lettuce and bean sprouts. Transfer rice to a serving bowl and garnish with Sichuan pepper and salt. Serve immediately.

Serve as a main for 2 or a side for 4

STIR-FRIED LAMB FILLETS WITH CARAMELISED RICE NOODLES

Lamb is eaten extensively in northern China. Combined with rice noodles, this tender marinated and stir-fried lamb makes for a delicious and substantial meal-in-a-bowl. Always buy the freshest rice noodles available and gently pull them apart before you stir-fry them – it's much harder to separate them once they're in the wok, as they tend to clump together. The ribbon-like rice noodles turn a deep golden-brown as they caramelise with the sugar, soy sauce and peanut oil. You can add a handful of coriander or Thai basil leaves along with the bean sprouts, if you like.

---

300 g lamb fillet, cut into 1 cm thick slices on the diagonal
500 g fresh rice noodle sheets
4 tablespoons peanut oil
2¼ teaspoons light soy sauce
2 tablespoons brown sugar
90 g (1 cup) bean sprouts
1 tablespoon roasted sesame seeds
1 lemon, halved

MARINADE
2 tablespoons shao hsing wine or dry sherry
1 tablespoon light soy sauce
1 teaspoon brown sugar
5 cm × 2 cm knob (20 g) ginger, cut into fine julienne strips
½ teaspoon sesame oil

Combine marinade ingredients in a bowl, add lamb and toss to coat well. Cover and leave to marinate in the refrigerator for 2 hours or overnight.

Cut block of rice noodles into 1.5 cm thick ribbons and gently pull apart to separate.

Heat 1 tablespoon oil in a hot wok until the surface seems to shimmer slightly. Add half of the marinated lamb and cook for 30 seconds each side to sear. Remove from wok with a slotted spoon. Repeat with another tablespoon of oil and the remaining lamb. Remove from wok and set aside.

Wipe wok clean and heat remaining 2 tablespoons oil until the surface seems to shimmer slightly. Add soy sauce and sugar and stir constantly for 30 seconds – the sauce will bubble up and caramelise. Add noodles to wok and stir-fry for 1½ minutes, tossing to coat in sauce and warm through.

Return lamb to wok and toss for 30 seconds or until warmed through. Remove from the heat, then add bean sprouts and toss through.

Arrange on a serving platter, garnish with roasted sesame seeds and squeeze over lemon juice to serve.

Serve as a main for 2

THIN EGG NOODLE SALAD WITH ROASTED PORK, PICKLED CARROT AND SESAME SEEDS

This recipe was inspired by my generous Uncle Jimmy, who always brings a huge tub of this along to family gatherings. Thin egg noodles are very delicate, and this light soy sauce and sesame dressing doesn't overwhelm them. If you are short of time, use BBQ pork and a jar of Chinese mixed pickles from Chinatown, but for a more glamorous version, use leftover Roasted Pork Shoulder with Miso and Honey (page 119).

---

500 g fresh thin egg noodles
1 tablespoon vegetable oil
250 g roasted pork, warm or at room temperature, cut into batons
1 tablespoon brown sugar
1 teaspoon light soy sauce
2 large sticks celery, finely sliced on the diagonal
90 g (1 cup) bean sprouts
60 g (½ cup) drained Pickled Carrot (page 253)
80 ml (⅓ cup) pickling liquid (from Pickled Carrot)
2 teaspoons sesame oil
2 tablespoons roasted sesame seeds

Bring a large saucepan of water to the boil. Blanch celery for 30 seconds, then remove with a slotted spoon. Refresh under cold running water and drain well. Pat dry.

Add vegetable oil to same pan of water and bring back to the boil. Add noodles and cook until al dente. Drain and refresh under cold water. Drain thoroughly and place in a large bowl.

Heat sugar and soy sauce in a non-stick frying pan until sugar has dissolved. Add pork and heat through for 45 seconds or until slightly sticky.

Add pork and remaining ingredients to noodles and toss well using your hands. Arrange on a platter to serve.

Serve as part of a banquet for 6–8

BEEF WITH CARAMELISED GLASS NOODLES AND PICKLED RED ONION

I am obsessed with glass noodles – I like to use them in soups, salads and stir-fries. Here the noodles are caramelised, giving them a deep colour and rich flavour.

450 g beef fillet, cut into 1 cm thick slices, then into 1 cm wide strips
100 g glass (bean thread) noodles
4 tablespoons peanut oil
1 tablespoon light soy sauce
1 tablespoon brown sugar
4 spring onions, finely sliced
2 teaspoons fish sauce
2 large red chillies, finely sliced

QUICK PICKLED RED ONION
1 small red onion, halved and finely sliced
1 teaspoon salt flakes
1 teaspoon white sugar
juice of 1 lemon

MARINADE
5 cm × 2 cm knob (20 g) ginger, finely diced
3 garlic cloves, finely diced
1 tablespoon light soy sauce
1 tablespoon shao hsing wine or dry sherry
1 tablespoon brown sugar
1 teaspoon malt vinegar
½ teaspoon sesame oil

To make the quick pickled red onion, place onion, salt and sugar in a bowl and combine well with your hands. Refrigerate for 30 minutes. Drain liquid from onion well and squeeze with your hands to remove any excess liquid, then toss with lemon juice just before serving.

Combine marinade ingredients in a bowl, add beef and toss to coat well. Cover and leave to marinate in the refrigerator for 30 minutes.

Soak noodles in hot tap water for 15 minutes, then drain thoroughly.

Heat 1 tablespoon oil in a hot wok until the surface seems to shimmer slightly. Add half of the beef and cook for 30 seconds to brown, then turn over and cook the other side for 10 seconds. Remove beef from wok using tongs and keep warm. Add another tablespoon of oil to wok and repeat with the remaining beef. Remove beef from wok and set aside with other beef.

Wipe wok clean and heat remaining 2 tablespoons oil until the surface seems to shimmer slightly. Add soy sauce and sugar and stir constantly for 30 seconds – the sauce will bubble up and caramelise. Add noodles to wok and stir-fry for 1 minute, tossing to coat in sauce and warm through.

Return beef to wok, add spring onion, fish sauce and half of the chilli and stir-fry for 30 seconds to warm beef through. Arrange in a serving bowl and garnish with pickled red onion and remaining chilli.

Serve as part of a banquet for 4–6

RICE NOODLES WITH GRILLED BEEF AND LEMON AND GINGER VINAIGRETTE

For the very best flavour, marinate the beef fillet overnight if possible. The oil needs to be very hot for stir-frying the rice noodles, in order to achieve the smoky, charred flavour of seared noodles that we all love; it's also very important not to keep tossing the noodles, but to let them sear on the base and sides of the wok.

---

1 × 300 g piece beef fillet, halved widthways
2 tablespoons vegetable oil, plus extra for brushing
500 g fresh rice noodle sheets
2 garlic cloves, crushed
5 cm × 3 cm knob (25 g) ginger, finely sliced
4 red shallots, quartered
2 teaspoons fish sauce
2 large or 4 small iceberg lettuce leaves, shredded
good pinch Sichuan Pepper and Salt (page 306)

MARINADE
2 tablespoons light soy sauce
2 tablespoons brown sugar
½ teaspoon malt vinegar
½ teaspoon sesame oil

LEMON AND GINGER VINAIGRETTE
5 cm × 2 cm knob (20 g) ginger, finely chopped
3 tablespoons lemon juice (from about 2 lemons)
½ teaspoon salt flakes
2 teaspoons light soy sauce
80 ml (⅓ cup) grapeseed oil

Combine marinade ingredients in a bowl, add beef and toss to coat well. Cover and leave to marinate in the refrigerator for 2 hours or overnight.

To make the vinaigrette, place ginger, lemon juice, salt and soy sauce in a bowl and whisk well to combine. While whisking, slowly drizzle in grapeseed oil and whisk to combine. Set aside until required, giving it another whisk just before using.

Heat a barbecue or chargrill pan to high. Lightly brush grill or pan with oil. Remove beef from marinade, discarding marinade. Grill beef for 2½ minutes, then turn over and grill for a further 1½ minutes for medium-rare. Transfer beef to a plate and leave to rest in a warm place for 5 minutes.

Meanwhile, cut block of rice noodles into 1.5 cm thick ribbons and gently pull apart to separate.

Heat oil in a wok until just smoking. Add garlic, ginger and shallot and cook, stirring occasionally, for 1 minute or until softened. Add noodles and cook for 3 minutes, only tossing every minute or so, until noodles are seared and hot. Add fish sauce and cook for 1 minute. Remove from the heat, then add lettuce and toss well.

Arrange noodles on a serving dish. Cut beef fillet into 5 mm thick slices and arrange over noodles. Pour over the resting juices from the beef, sprinkle with Sichuan pepper and salt and serve with a side dish of lemon and ginger vinaigrette for dipping.

Serve as a main for 2

STIR-FRIED HOKKIEN NOODLES WITH CHILLI SAUCE AND CHINESE CABBAGE

Because Hokkien noodles are so robust and meaty in their texture, I like to team them with rich sauces, such as this chilli sauce. The secret to getting seared, super-hot noodles is not to play with them too much, allowing them to remain in contact with the wok. The cool, crunchy cabbage in this recipe is a welcome contrast to the spicy, hot noodles. For a change, you could make this dish with XO Sauce (page 298), or try adding bean sprouts and shredded iceberg lettuce at the same time as the cabbage.

3 tablespoons Chilli Sauce (page 297)
1¼ tablespoons light soy sauce
1 teaspoon sesame oil
2 large red chillies
2 tablespoons peanut oil
2 spring onions, cut into 10 cm lengths
1 small red onion, cut into quarters
5 cm × 3 cm knob (25 g) ginger, finely sliced
500 g fresh Hokkien noodles
3 Chinese cabbage leaves, finely shredded
pinch Sichuan Pepper and Salt (page 306)

Combine chilli sauce, soy sauce and sesame oil in a bowl and set aside.

Trim stems off chillies, cut in half lengthways and remove seeds with a spoon.

Heat peanut oil in a hot wok until the surface seems to shimmer slightly. Add chilli halves and cook for 30 seconds each side to blister and slightly blacken. Remove with tongs and drain on kitchen paper. Reserve oil in wok.

Add spring onion, red onion and ginger to wok and cook for 2 minutes or until onion is lightly caramelised.

Add noodles and cook for 4 minutes, only tossing every minute or so, until noodles are seared and hot.

Next add chilli sauce mixture and stir-fry for 1 minute, tossing noodles to coat them in the sauce.

Add cabbage and toss for 30 seconds to combine. Transfer to a serving platter and garnish with blistered chillies and Sichuan pepper and salt.

Serve as a main for 2 or as part of a banquet for 2–4

SCALLOP AND GINGER DUMPLINGS WITH CHILLI–VINEGAR DIPPING SAUCE

This recipe allows you to enjoy freshly made Chinese-style dumplings without all the fuss of making and rolling your own dough. I simply buy a packet of fresh wonton wrappers from a Chinese grocery store and wrap them around this delicious filling. You could substitute the scallop flesh with freshly picked crabmeat or prawn meat, perhaps also adding some chopped coriander and mint. It's really best to make the dumplings on the day you wish to eat them, since they get soggy if left overnight in the refrigerator.

16 fresh scallops (180 g), halved crossways
2 spring onions, finely sliced
5 cm × 1 cm knob (15 g) ginger, finely diced
1 teaspoon light soy sauce
½ teaspoon white sugar
½ teaspoon sesame oil
16 fresh wonton wrappers (about 8 cm square)
125 ml (½ cup) Chilli-Vinegar Dipping Sauce (page 302)

Combine all ingredients except wonton wrappers and dipping sauce in a bowl.

Next, fill and shape the dumplings (page 286).

Bring a large saucepan of water to the boil. Drop dumplings into the water and boil for 2½ minutes or until cooked and wrappers are translucent. To test if the dumplings are ready, you will need to remove one and cut into it with a sharp knife to check that the filling is hot. When ready, remove with a slotted spoon and drain on a plate.

Arrange dumplings on a platter and serve immediately with a side dish of dipping sauce.

Serve as a starter for 4

VEGETABLE DUMPLINGS WITH GINGER–VINEGAR DIPPING SAUCE

I love the filling in these dumplings – the initial salting of the cabbage is a traditional way of drawing excess moisture out of the cabbage and intensifying its flavour. Cooking the mushrooms with the aromatics also heightens the flavour, making for an extremely delicious filling.

---

200 g Chinese cabbage (about 4 leaves), finely shredded
2 teaspoons salt flakes
2 teaspoons light soy sauce
½ teaspoon white sugar
½ teaspoon sesame oil
50 g oyster mushrooms, trimmed and finely diced
3 Braised Chinese Mushrooms (page 220), finely diced
5 cm × 5 cm knob (35 g) ginger, finely diced
¼ bunch garlic chives, finely chopped
2 spring onions, finely sliced
½ bunch coriander, stems only, finely sliced
1 tablespoon peanut oil
16 fresh wonton wrappers (about 8 cm square)
125 ml (½ cup) Ginger–Vinegar Dipping Sauce (page 302)

Combine cabbage and salt in a bowl. Mix well, using your hands, and leave covered in the refrigerator for 1 hour.

Meanwhile, combine soy sauce, sugar and sesame oil in a bowl.

Combine all of the mushrooms, ginger, garlic chives, spring onions and coriander stems in a bowl. Heat oil in a hot wok until the surface seems to shimmer slightly. Add mushroom mixture and stir-fry for 30 seconds. Add soy sauce mixture and stir-fry for 1 minute. Transfer to a large bowl, spreading the mixture out over the base so it will cool quickly, then refrigerate until chilled.

Drain liquid from salted cabbage and squeeze well with your hands – if the filling is too wet, it will make the dumplings soggy. Add to mushroom mixture and mix thoroughly.

Next, fill and shape the dumplings (page 286).

Bring a large saucepan of water to the boil. Drop dumplings into the water and boil for 2½ minutes or until wrappers are transparent and cooked. Remove with a slotted spoon and drain on a plate. Serve immediately with a side dish of dipping sauce.

Serve as a starter for 4

FILLING AND SHAPING WONTONS

❶ Place a rounded teaspoon of filling in the centre of a wonton wrapper.

❷ Dip your finger in water and moisten the edges of the wrapper.

❸ Fold the wrapper in half over the filling, creating a rectangle. Lightly press around filling and along edges to seal.

FILLING AND SHAPING DUMPLINGS

❶ Place a rounded teaspoon of the filling in the centre of a wrapper.

❷ Dip your finger in water and moisten the edges of the wrapper.

❸ Gently lift one corner of the wrapper.

❹ Hold the wonton lengthways in between your hands and fold the sealed edge of the wonton back in on itself,

❺ Lightly moisten one corner of the folded edge with water. Take the two ends in your fingers, bring them together with a twisting action and press lightly to join.

❻ Repeat with remaining wrappers and filling.

❹ Fold the wrapper in half over the filling, creating a triangle.

❺ Lightly press around filling and along edges to seal.

❻ Repeat with remaining wrappers and filling.

DEEP-FRIED SCALLOP AND GINGER WONTONS

Although the filling in this recipe is similar to that used in the Scallop and Ginger Dumplings on page 282, the wrapping technique is the traditional one used for wontons (page 286). Eat these straightaway, while they are hot and super-crunchy, or serve them in a soup (page 62), if you prefer.

---

vegetable oil, for deep-frying

SCALLOP AND GINGER WONTONS
- **180 g fresh scallop meat (about 16 scallops), roughly chopped**
- **2 spring onions, finely sliced**
- **5 cm × 1 cm knob (15 g) ginger, finely diced**
- **1 teaspoon light soy sauce**
- **½ teaspoon white sugar**
- **½ teaspoon sesame oil**
- **16 fresh wonton wrappers (about 8 cm square)**

DIPPING SAUCE
- **3 teaspoons peanut oil**
- **3 cm × 1 cm knob (15 g) ginger, finely diced**
- **2 garlic cloves, finely diced**
- **80 ml (⅓ cup) white vinegar**
- **2 tablespoons white sugar**
- **1 teaspoon light soy sauce**

To make the dipping sauce, heat peanut oil in a hot wok, add ginger and garlic and stir-fry for 30 seconds. Add vinegar and sugar and cook for 1 minute, then remove from heat. Stir in soy sauce and set aside until ready to serve.

To make the scallop and ginger wontons, combine all ingredients except wonton wrappers in a bowl.

Next, fill and shape the wontons (page 286).

Pour enough oil for deep-frying into a wok and heat until the surface seems to shimmer slightly (190°C). Add wontons, in batches, and deep-fry for about 1 minute or until golden and puffed up. To test if the wontons are ready, you will need to remove one and cut into it with a sharp knife to check that the filling is hot. When ready, remove with tongs and drain on a kitchen paper. Repeat the process with the remaining wontons.

Arrange on a platter and serve immediately with a side dish of dipping sauce.

Serve as a starter for 4

SAUCES AND SALTS

GINGER SAUCE (LEFT)

This beautiful, aromatic, super-tasty sauce is quick to make. It can be served with chicken or seafood, or alongside a dish of noodles. Often I have it just with a bowl of steamed rice.

90 g ginger, finely diced (about ¾ cup diced ginger)
1½ teaspoons salt flakes
80 ml (⅓ cup) peanut oil

Combine ginger and salt in a small heatproof bowl and spread evenly over the base – this will ensure that the hot oil is well absorbed.

Heat oil in a small saucepan until the surface seems to shimmer slightly (if the oil begins to smoke, it is too hot – let it cool for a minute or two). Carefully pour the hot oil over the ginger mix to scald. Stir well to combine, then set aside until ready to use.

This sauce can be stored in an airtight container in the refrigerator for up to 1 day, but should be brought back to room temperature before serving.

Makes 250 ml (1 cup)

SPRING ONION–GINGER SAUCE (RIGHT)

Everyone seems to love this – it's delicious served with poached chicken, steamed prawns, lobster or fish. The secret lies in scalding the aromatics with hot peanut oil, giving the sauce a nutty, smoky flavour. If you are allergic to peanuts, try using vegetable oil with a dash of sesame oil instead.

2 spring onions, finely sliced
80 g ginger, finely diced (about ⅔ cup diced ginger)
2 teaspoons salt flakes
125 ml (½ cup) peanut oil

Combine spring onion, ginger and salt in a heatproof bowl and spread evenly over the base – this will ensure that the hot oil is well absorbed.

Heat oil in a small saucepan until the surface seems to shimmer slightly (if the oil begins to smoke, it is too hot – let it cool for a minute or two). Carefully pour the hot oil over the spring onion-ginger mix to scald. Stir well to combine, then set aside until ready to use.

This sauce can be stored in an airtight container in the refrigerator for up to 1 day, but should be brought back to room temperature before serving.

Makes 250 ml (1 cup)

Use in • Poached Lobster with Spring Onion–Ginger Sauce (page 165)

CARAMEL SPICED SOY SAUCE (LEFT)

This is a very simple yet intensely flavoured sauce. In addition to the uses given below, it works well as a dipping sauce with any meat or poultry, with grilled or roasted ocean trout or salmon, or with deep-fried snapper.

220 g (1 cup) white sugar
145 ml light soy sauce
1 cinnamon quill
1 star anise
5 cm × 1 cm knob (15 g) ginger, thickly sliced
2 tablespoons malt vinegar

Place sugar and soy sauce in a small saucepan and bring to the boil, stirring to dissolve sugar. Add cinnamon, star anise, ginger and vinegar, reduce heat to low–medium and simmer for 6 minutes or until caramelised and slightly syrupy.

Remove from heat and leave to infuse for 1 hour, then discard cinnamon and star anise. Store in an airtight container in the refrigerator for up to 1 week.

Makes 250 ml (1 cup)

Use in • Braised Silken Tofu with Caramel Spiced Soy Sauce and Deep-Fried Garlic Slices (page 219)
• Home-Style Fried Eggs with Roasted Pork (page 177)

SPRING ONION–CHILLI SAUCE (RIGHT)

A simple dipping sauce that goes well with anything and everything. Omit the peanut oil if you are allergic, and use vegetable oil instead.

2 spring onions, finely sliced
1–2 large red chillies, finely sliced
3 tablespoons light soy sauce
½ teaspoon sesame oil
1 tablespoon peanut oil

Combine spring onion, chilli, soy sauce and sesame oil in a heatproof bowl and spread evenly over base – this will ensure that the hot oil is well absorbed.

Heat peanut oil in a small saucepan until the surface seems to shimmer slightly (if the oil begins to smoke, it is too hot – let it cool for a minute or two). Carefully pour the hot oil over the spring onion-chilli mix to scald. Stir well to combine, then set aside until ready to use.

This sauce can be stored in an airtight container in the refrigerator for up to 1 day, but should be brought back to room temperature before serving.

Makes about 180 ml (¾ cup)

Use in • Stir-fried Omelette with Snow Peas, Herbs and Bean Sprouts (page 181)

SWEET CHILLI SAUCE (LEFT)

This sauce is really Vietnamese or Thai in style, rather than strictly Chinese. Its rich taste and nectar-like texture work especially well with deep-fried foods. I like to balance out its sweetness with some fish sauce, and you could always add a big squeeze of lemon or lime for extra tanginess. As well as the uses given below, it would be fabulous served alongside Stir-Fried Lamb Fillets with Caramelised Rice Noodles (page 273), with Deep-fried Scallop and Ginger Wontons (page 288), or just with grilled ocean trout or prawns.

250 ml (1 cup) white vinegar
165 g (¾ cup) white sugar
2½ tablespoons fish sauce
1 large red chilli, finely sliced

Place vinegar and sugar in a small heavy-based saucepan and bring to the boil, stirring to dissolve sugar.

Reduce heat and simmer, uncovered, for about 10 minutes or until liquid is reduced by almost half and slightly syrupy. Remove from heat and allow to cool, then stir in fish sauce and chilli. Set aside until required. Store in an airtight container in the refrigerator for up to 1 week.

Makes 250 ml (1 cup)

Use in
- Chicken and Bean Curd Rolls (page 81)
- Vegetarian Spring Rolls (page 195)

CHILLI SAUCE (RIGHT)

There is nothing better than making your own chilli sauce, rather than having to make do with artificial-tasting, gloopy versions out of a bottle – and you can make it as hot or as mild as you wish. Larger chillies are generally milder and sweeter in flavour, while smaller chillies can be super-hot. I serve this with almost everything!

8 large red chillies, roughly chopped
6 garlic cloves, roughly chopped
75 g ginger, roughly chopped
125 ml (½ cup) peanut oil
½ teaspoon brown sugar
1 tablespoon light soy sauce

Process chilli, garlic and ginger in a food processor or blender until finely chopped.

Heat oil in a wok until the surface seems to shimmer slightly. Reduce heat to low–medium, add chilli, garlic and ginger and cook, stirring regularly, for about 3 minutes to cook out the flavours.

Add sugar and cook for 1 minute, stirring regularly so the sauce doesn't catch on the base of the wok.

Stir through soy sauce, reduce heat to low and cook, still stirring, for 10 minutes – the sauce should darken in colour and the oil should leach out at this stage. The chilli sauce can be used straightaway or cooled and stored in an airtight container in the refrigerator for up to 1 week.

Makes 240 g (1 cup)

Use in
- Barbecued Pork Ribs (page 123)
- Steamed Lobster with Chilli Sauce (page 168)
- Stir-fried Potato with Chilli Sauce and Black Beans (page 203)
- Stir-fried Hokkien Noodles with Chilli Sauce and Chinese Cabbage (page 281)

XO SAUCE

XO sauce is a relatively recent addition to the Chinese repertoire, and is an oily, powerful-tasting, intensely textured, garlicky chilli paste. The small dried red chillies are optional, but I like the extra heat and the smoky, dark quality they add. Do take care when blistering them – they turn black very quickly, and must be removed at once. If they blacken too much, simply discard them and start again; otherwise, they will add a burnt taint that will ruin the sauce. A generous amount of oil is needed for this sauce, to allow for the slow-cooking of all the ingredients without any of them catching on the bottom of the wok and burning. I serve a small bowl of XO sauce alongside meals; it also makes a good dipping sauce for boiled dumplings.

55 g (½ cup) dried shrimps
80 g (½ cup) dried scallops
250 ml (1 cup) shao hsing wine or dry sherry
11 large red chillies, roughly chopped
7 garlic cloves, roughly chopped
2 large red shallots, roughly chopped
375 ml (1½ cups) peanut oil
3 dried small red chillies
55 g smoked bacon, rind removed but fat left on, finely diced
3 teaspoons light soy sauce
1 teaspoon brown sugar

Place dried shrimps in a small bowl and cover with half of the wine or sherry. Place dried scallops in another, medium-sized bowl and cover with remaining half of the wine or sherry. The liquid needs to completely cover the shrimps and scallops – transfer to more appropriately sized bowls if it doesn't. Cover with cling wrap and leave in refrigerator overnight.

The next day, drain shrimps and reserve liquid. Drain scallops and reserve liquid. Mix shrimps and scallops together, place in a food processor and process until finely shredded. Remove and set aside. Place large red chilli, garlic and shallot in food processor and process until finely chopped. Remove and set aside.

Heat peanut oil in a hot wok until the surface seems to shimmer slightly. Add dried chillies and cook for 30 seconds each side to blister and slightly blacken. Remove chillies with a slotted spoon and drain on kitchen paper. Reserve oil in wok.

Reduce heat to medium, carefully add chilli, garlic and shallot mixture and bacon to oil. Simmer, stirring regularly, for 3 minutes to cook out the flavours.

Next add shrimp and scallop mixture and cook for 6 minutes, stirring regularly so the sauce doesn't catch on the base of the wok – the oil should leach out at this stage.

Add the reserved soaking liquid from both the shrimps and scallops. Stir gently for 3 minutes to cook out the wine, then reduce heat to low and simmer, stirring occasionally, for 15 minutes.

Add soy sauce, sugar and the blistered dried chillies and cook for 2 minutes.

Remove from heat and allow to cool. The XO sauce can be used straightaway or cooled and stored in an airtight container in the refrigerator for up to 1 month – the flavours will intensify over this time. If serving as a condiment, be sure to remove the required amount from the refrigerator 30 minutes before serving.

Makes 700 g (3 cups)

Use in
- Stir-fried Scallops with XO Sauce (page 142)
- Stir-fried Iceberg Lettuce with XO Sauce (page 204)
- Fried Rice with XO Sauce (page 270)

GARLIC–SOY DIPPING SAUCE (LEFT)

A light, flavoursome dipping sauce that works well with dumplings, poultry, pork and seafood.

3 garlic cloves, finely diced
2 tablespoons light soy sauce
1 teaspoon malt vinegar
½ teaspoon sesame oil

Place all ingredients in a small bowl and combine well. Set aside until required.

Makes 80 ml (⅓ cup)

CHILLI–SOY DIPPING SAUCE (RIGHT)

A super-simple dipping sauce that goes with almost everything. In my restaurant I serve this alongside a small dish of Chilli Sauce (page 297), so people have the choice of raw or cooked chilli.

1 large red chilli, finely sliced
3 tablespoons light soy sauce
½ teaspoon sesame oil

Place ingredients in a small bowl and combine well. Set aside until required.

Makes 80 ml (⅓ cup)

Use in
- Quail with Chilli–Soy Dipping Sauce and Pickled Cucumber (page 78)
- White-Cooked Pork Belly with Pickles and Blistered Chillies (page 108)
- Crab and Zucchini Cakes with Chilli–Soy Dipping Sauce (page 162)
- Crispy Tofu with Fish Stuffing (page 216)

GINGER–VINEGAR DIPPING SAUCE (TOP)

Traditionally served with dumplings, this sauce is fine and delicate.

---

5 cm × 2 cm knob (20 g) ginger, cut into fine julienne strips
80 ml (⅓ cup) malt vinegar

Place ingredients in a small bowl and combine well. Set aside until required.

Makes 125 ml (½ cup)

Use in • Vegetable Dumplings with Ginger–Vinegar Dipping Sauce (page 285)

CHILLI–VINEGAR DIPPING SAUCE (LEFT)

I serve this with scallop and ginger dumplings and crispy prawn cakes – it's quite light and delicate.

---

1 large red chilli, finely sliced
2 tablespoons light soy sauce
3 tablespoons malt vinegar

Place ingredients in a small bowl and combine well. Set aside until required.

Makes 125 ml (½ cup)

Use in • Crispy Prawn Cakes with Chilli–Vinegar Dipping Sauce (page 138)
• Scallop and Ginger Dumplings with Chilli–Vinegar Dipping Sauce (page 282)

GARLIC–VINEGAR DIPPING SAUCE (RIGHT)

This is a perfect dipping sauce for dumplings. It also goes well with poached quail or white-cooked pork belly.

---

4 garlic cloves, finely diced
3 tablespoons malt vinegar

Place ingredients in a small bowl and combine well. Set aside until required.

Makes 80 ml (⅓ cup)

SPICY SALT (LEFT)

A really simply made salt that is packed with flavour and aroma, this will turn an ordinary dish into an exotic, utterly mouth-watering one. Include it in a marinade for lamb or beef, sprinkle it over grilled ocean trout or prawns, or use to season roast winter vegetables.

1 teaspoon Sichuan peppercorns
1 teaspoon fennel seeds
1 teaspoon coriander seeds
1 teaspoon cumin seeds
2 tablespoons salt flakes

Combine all ingredients in a heavy-based frying pan and dry-roast over medium heat, tossing occasionally. When the peppercorns begin to pop and become aromatic, about 1–2 minutes, take off the heat.

Allow to cool, then coarsely grind using a mortar and pestle or spice grinder. Store in an airtight container for several weeks.

Makes 2½ tablespoons

Use in
• Crispy-Skin Chicken with Spicy Salt and Lemon (page 70)
• Salad of Prawns, Pickled Cauliflower, Pickled Red Onion and Black Cloud Ear Fungus (page 233)

CHILLI SALT (RIGHT)

Another great, simply made but very tasty salt that works particularly well with seafood and poultry. This goes with so many dishes that I keep it on my dinner table next to the ordinary salt, as I like a touch of chilli on most things.

2 teaspoons dried chilli flakes
2 tablespoons salt flakes

Combine all ingredients in a heavy-based frying pan and dry-roast over medium heat, tossing occasionally. When the salt changes colour and the mixture becomes aromatic, about 1–2 minutes, take off the heat.

Allow to cool, then coarsely grind using a mortar and pestle or spice grinder. Store in an airtight container for several weeks.

Makes 1½ tablespoons

Use in
• Fried Oysters with Chilli Salt and Pickled Red Onion (page 137)
• Deep-Fried School Prawns with Chilli Salt and Lemon (page 146)
• Deep-Fried Soft-Boiled Eggs with Iceberg Lettuce and Chilli Salt (page 185)
• Salad of Red-Braised Poussin, Black Cloud Ear Fungus and Celery (page 238)

SICHUAN PEPPER AND SALT

As you can see, I use this extensively in my recipes – the numbing, tingly, woody, aromatic and mysterious flavour of this salt is addictive. It is at its most potent and zingy when made fresh, so do try and make it when you need it, rather than making enough to last a year!

1 tablespoon Sichuan peppercorns

3 tablespoons salt flakes

Combine all ingredients in a heavy-based frying pan and dry-roast over medium heat, tossing occasionally. When the peppercorns begin to pop and become aromatic, about 1–2 minutes, take off the heat.

Allow to cool, then coarsely grind using a mortar and pestle or spice grinder. Store in an airtight container for several weeks.

Makes 2¼ tablespoons

Use in

- Crispy Orange-Peel Beef (page 100)
- Barbecued Pork Ribs (page 123)
- Sashimi of Snapper with Chilli–Lime Dressing (page 130)
- Stir-fried Scallops with XO Sauce (page 142)
- Steamed Mussels with Sichuan Chilli Oil and Pickled Celery (page 150)
- Grilled Marinated Squid (page 161)
- Stir-fried Potato with Chilli Sauce and Black Beans (page 203)
- Stir-fried Iceberg Lettuce with XO Sauce (page 204)
- Braised Silken Tofu with Caramel Spiced Soy Sauce and Deep-Fried Garlic Slices (page 219)
- Salad of Chinese Cabbage, Bok Choy and Fennel with Tomato Dressing (page 229)
- Salad of Jellyfish with Vinegar and Sesame Dressing (page 234)
- Fried Rice with XO Sauce (page 270)
- Rice Noodles with Grilled Beef and Lemon and Ginger Vinaigrette (page 278)
- Stir-fried Hokkien Noodles with Chilli Sauce and Chinese Cabbage (page 281)

ACKNOWLEDGEMENTS

Creating this book has been an absolute privilege, for I've had the opportunity to work alongside so many talented, caring, professional and highly gifted people: Julie Gibbs, my creative and dynamic publisher; Daniel New, a graphic designer with great vision, no boundaries and a sensitive heart; Alison Cowan, my long-time editor extraordinaire; Earl Carter, master photographer, artist and friend; Belinda So, the best recipe tester in this country; and Matt Page and Jessica Smede, who, with a keen eye for detail, sourced beautiful props for the photography. With special thanks also to Clio Kempster for producing the photo shoot, Nicole Abadee and Ellen Harvey for editorial assistance, and Tracey Jarrett for production. As always, my enormous gratitude and respect go to the whole Penguin team, for being so supportive and encouraging over the years.

Endless love, appreciation and thanks to my entire Billy Kwong crew, for their patience, hard work and beautiful, heart-felt cooking and service; and, most of all, to my completely wonderful, original and inspiring Nell, and to my family, for always being there every step of the way, thank you.

INDEX

Ten crowd-pleasers

C

Ten meals-in-a-bowl

G

Six weeknight stir-fries

P

Q

R

Six winter soups and braises

S

Something special

LANTERN

Published by the Penguin Group
Penguin Group (Australia)
250 Camberwell Road, Camberwell, Victoria 3124, Australia
(a division of Pearson Australia Group Pty Ltd)
Penguin Group (USA) Inc.
375 Hudson Street, New York, New York 10014, USA
Penguin Group (Canada)
90 Eglinton Avenue East, Suite 700, Toronto, Canada ON M4P 2Y3
(a division of Pearson Penguin Canada Inc.)
Penguin Books Ltd
80 Strand, London WC2R 0RL England
Penguin Ireland
25 St Stephen's Green, Dublin 2, Ireland
(a division of Penguin Books Ltd)
Penguin Books India Pvt Ltd
11 Community Centre, Panchsheel Park, New Delhi – 110 017, India
Penguin Group (NZ)
67 Apollo Drive, Rosedale, North Shore 0632, New Zealand
(a division of Pearson New Zealand Ltd)
Penguin Books (South Africa) (Pty) Ltd
24 Sturdee Avenue, Rosebank, Johannesburg 2196, South Africa

Penguin Books Ltd, Registered Offices: 80 Strand, London, WC2R 0RL, England

First published by Penguin Group (Australia), 2012

10 9 8 7 6 5 4 3 2 1

Designed by Daniel New © Penguin Group (Australia)
Propping by Matt Page and Jessica Smede
Typeset in Archer by Post Pre-press Group, Brisbane, Queensland
Colour reproduction by Splitting Image, Clayton, Victoria
Printed and bound in Singapore by Imago

National Library of Australia
Cataloguing-in-Publication entry:

Kwong, Kylie
Kylie Kwong's simple chinese cooking class / Kylie Kwong ;
photographed by Earl Carter.
ISBN: 9781920989675 (hbk.)
Includes index.
Cooking, Chinese.
Carter, Earl, 1957-

641.5951

penguin.com.au/lantern